D0927740

KILL HITLER

Operation *Valkyrie* 1944

NEIL SHORT

First published in Great Britain in 2013 by Osprey Publishing,
Midland House, West Way, Botley, Oxford, OX2 0PH, UK
43-01 21st Street, Suite 220B, Long Island City, NY 11101
E-mail: info@ospreypublishing.com

Osprey Publishing is part of the Osprey Group

A CIP catalogue record for this book is available from the British Library

Print ISBN: 978 1 78096 258 0
PDF ebook ISBN: 978 1 78096 259 7
ePub ebook ISBN: 978 1 78096 260 3

Index by Zoe Ross
Typeset in Sabon
Maps by Bounford.com
BEV by Adam Hook; originally published in FOR 100 *The Führer's
Headquarters*
Originated by PDQ Media, Bungay, UK
Printed in China through Worldprint

13 14 15 16 17   10 9 8 7 6 5 4 3 2 1

Osprey Publishing is supporting the Woodland Trust, the UK's leading
woodland conservation charity, by funding the dedication of trees.

www.ospreypublishing.com

DEDICATION

This book is dedicated to the memory of the many members of the
German resistance who perished before, during and after the 20 July Plot.
That you were unsuccessful in overthrowing the Nazi tyranny is immaterial
– you tried.

ACKNOWLEDGEMENTS

I would like to thank all those people who helped in the production of this
book. I am particularly grateful to Steve Zaloga, for providing copies of
images from the US National Archives, and Ian Whalley, for the contacts he
gave me. Finally, I would like to thank my wife and children for their
support and patience. None of this would be possible without you.

ARTIST'S NOTE

Readers may care to note that the original paintings from which the
battlescenes of this book were prepared are available for private sale. All
reproduction copyright whatsoever is retained by the Publishers. All
inquiries should be addressed to:

Peter Dennis, 'Fieldhead', The Park, Mansfield, Nottinghamshire NG18 2AT,
UK, or email magie.h@ntlworld.com

The Publishers regret that they can enter into no correspondence upon
this matter.

EDITOR'S NOTE

For ease of comparison please refer to the following conversion table:

1 mile = 1.6km
1yd = 0.9m
1ft = 0.3m
1in = 2.54cm/25.4mm

COMPARATIVE OFFICER RANKS

Heer	Luftwaffe	Kriegsmarine	Waffen-SS	British Army
n/a	Reichsmarschall	n/a	Reichführer-SS	n/a
Generalfeldmarschall	Generalfeldmarschall	Grossadmiral	n/a	Field Marshal
Generaloberst	Generaloberst	Generaladmiral	SS-Oberstgruppenführer	General
General der Infanterie, etc.	General der Flieger, etc.	Admiral	SS-Obergruppenführer	Lieutenant-General
Generalleutnant	Generalleutnant	Vizeadmiral	SS-Gruppenführer	Major-General
Generalmajor	Generalmajor	Konteradmiral	SS-Brigadeführer	Brigadier
n/a	n/a	Kommodore	SS-Oberführer	n/a
Oberst	Oberst	Kapitän zur See	SS-Standartenführer	Colonel
Oberstleutnant	Oberstleutnant	Fregattenkapitän	SS-Obersturmbannführer	Lieutenant-Colonel
Major	Major	Korvettenkapitän	SS-Sturmbannführer	Major
Hauptmann/Rittmeister	Hauptmann	Kapitänleutnant	SS-Hauptsturmführer	Captain
Oberleutnant	Oberleutnant	Oberleutnant zur See	SS-Obersturmführer	Lieutenant
Leutnant	Leutnant	Leutnant zur See	SS-Untersturmführer	Second Lieutenant

CONTENTS

INTRODUCTION

On 20 July 1944 a group of disaffected German Army officers launched one of the most daring undertakings of World War II: an attempt to kill Adolf Hitler at the Wolfsschanze (Wolf's Lair), the Führer's East Prussian headquarters. The operation was daring because security around Hitler was extremely tight, which befitted a man who was almost universally hated and who was paranoid about assassination – or worse, being captured by his enemies. The Führer's movements were a closely guarded secret, although in truth, by this stage in the war, Hitler rarely left his concrete bunker at the Wolfsschanze. Hitler had designed the bunker himself and it was proof against the heaviest Allied bombs. Around it were a series of barbed-wire fences; beyond these were minefields and roadblocks. Elite troops were hand-picked for his personal security and additional heavily armed troops patrolled the perimeter of the headquarters or were stationed on roads leading to it.

The raid was not only daring in terms of the physical dangers it presented, it was also unique, as the conspirators were planning to assassinate the leader of a major world power. Moreover, Hitler was the 'legally' elected leader of Germany and a man to whom they had sworn an oath of allegiance. This meant their actions were treasonable, and each man knew that if the assassination attempt failed they would face the ultimate sanction. Bad luck and a quick and ruthless response from the Nazi leadership, which stood in stark contrast to the ponderous and often half-hearted actions of the plotters, meant the operation foundered and most of the conspirators died, either by their own hands or by execution following a demeaning show trial.

Although the 20 July Plot is by far the best-known attempt on Hitler's life, with countless books on the subject and Hollywood adaptations, the army had in fact planned to arrest or kill Hitler on a number of occasions. As early as 1938, before the war in Europe had started, several senior officers sought to remove Hitler from power, with the support of the Western democracies. The appeasement of Hitler put paid to this attempt, but did not entirely extinguish the fire and an effort was made to resurrect the plan before the invasion of France in 1940. This time the resolve of the army's leadership failed. Continental Europe was overrun and many in Germany, including the army, were now intoxicated by the seemingly unending victories. Resistance based on moral repugnance continued, but it was not until the tide of the war began to turn that serious consideration was again given to removing Hitler. There were attempts to shoot him, blow up his plane and even use a suicide bomber, but none succeeded.

By July 1944 the plotters were getting desperate. The Allies had landed in Normandy and a number of key figures in the resistance had been arrested. It was now or never. With others either unwilling or unable to undertake the task, a young officer, Oberst Claus Schenk Graf von Stauffenberg, a wounded veteran of the North African campaign, undertook to kill Hitler. On 20 July 1944 he flew to the Wolfsschanze, ostensibly to brief Hitler on the state of the Ersatzheer (Replacement Army). On entering the briefing room, he secreted a bomb before making his exit. At 1242hrs it detonated, severely damaging the briefing room, killing four people and injuring many more. Miraculously, Hitler survived and was ushered to safety.

A view of the devastated briefing room after the bomb exploded. The heavy table on which the maps were spread and which helped save Hitler's life is in the foreground. Also visible are a number of stools that were stored under the table. (NARA)

**Adolf Hitler
becomes Chancellor
of Germany**

**Beck writes to
Hitler condemning
his aggressive
foreign policy**

Front elevation of the
Bendlerblock as it looks
today. It overlooks the
Landwehrkanal, which
links to the River Spree.
The building was the
headquarters of
the Replacement Army
during World War II and
is still used by the
German Ministry of
Defence. (Author)

Yet, although the Führer had survived, the conspirators still had a chance of overthrowing the regime. Stauffenberg returned to Berlin and mobilized troops in the city and further afield. Under the auspices of Operation *Valkyrie* – emergency powers that had been drawn up to deal with internal unrest – key buildings were seized and individuals loyal to the regime were arrested. Communication links to the Wolfsschanze had also been disrupted, but had not been completely cut. Consequently, Hitler and his cohorts were aware of the coup attempt in Berlin and were able to take steps to crush it and deliver their own message over the radio to the German people. As the news of Hitler's survival filtered out, the coup gradually lost momentum. By late evening it was clear that the attempt had failed.

Those involved with the plot were tried and executed. In the following days and weeks the net was cast much wider, and anyone associated with the resistance was rounded up. In the end it is believed that some 4,000 people were executed. However, the fallout from the 20 July Plot went much further. The conspiracy among senior officers was used to explain

the reverses at the front and, increasingly, Hitler placed his faith in officers from the Kriegsmarine (navy) and Luftwaffe (air force), even though these branches of the armed forces were largely irrelevant in the final days of the war. The Wehrmacht (German armed forces) was purged, senior officers were removed and replaced by more trustworthy, but often less capable, officers and, in a final humiliation, the military salute was replaced by the Nazi salute. Politically, Himmler's power grew. He was put in charge of the replacement army and was responsible for raising a new 'people's' army (the new *Volk* units), which was commanded by SS officers and reported through the SS chain of command. Paradoxically, although Himmler's power grew, these new responsibilities took him away from the Führer and, arguably, the major benefactor was Martin Bormann, who, as private secretary, controlled access to Hitler.

At a personal level the plot had enormous ramifications, and not just for those involved in the coup. The families of those executed or incarcerated not only suffered personal loss; in many cases they were placed under house arrest and, thereafter, their every action was viewed with suspicion. Hitler himself, although the physical injuries he received on 20 July were relatively minor, was clearly shaken by the experience and had deep psychological scars. They served to deepen his paranoia and his leadership became increasingly erratic until, on 30 April 1945, he took his own life.

Plötzensee Prison in Berlin where many of the conspirators were executed. The door to the left leads to a memorial and the door to the right leads to a small exhibition that includes a history of the prison and details those who were put to death there, including the victims rounded up after 20 July. (Author)

ORIGINS

The roots of resistance

To understand the origins of the 20 July Plot, it is necessary first to say a few words about the way in which Hitler and the National Socialists (Nazis) gained power in Germany, and the origins of the widespread opposition to their rule. Although never securing a democratic majority, the Nazis managed to turn Germany into an authoritarian state through emergency laws, enabling acts and plebiscites. This so-called 'legal revolution' was particularly difficult for the political Left to challenge. The trades unions, the Socialists and the Communists had an opportunity to unseat the Nazis in 1933, while their respective organizations were still relatively strong. However, lack of a common aim and mutual mistrust meant that it was impossible to establish a unified 'Left'. This was certainly not helped by the KPD (Kommunistische Partei Deutschlands – German Communist Party), which fought the Nazis on the streets, but also attacked the Socialists because of their desire to seek power through the ballot box.

This inability to produce a consensus proved disastrous. In May 1933 the trades unions were dissolved and, in July 1933, all political parties were outlawed. A number of prominent left-wing leaders fled the country and sought to effect change from without. Those that stayed established underground groups, but these were ruthlessly crushed by the Gestapo (Geheime Staatspolizei – Secret State Police) and any remaining hope that a Communist-led government would gain popular support was extinguished by the Nazi–Soviet Pact of 23 August 1939. The attack on the Soviet Union in 22 June 1941 provided a glimmer of hope, but the war against the Bolsheviks brought greater surveillance and persecution of the Communists within Germany and meant there was little chance to coordinate opposition.

The opposition offered by the Left was therefore divided and unable to establish a united movement capable of confronting the Nazis. This was not the case with the Church, but for a number of reasons it, too, failed to

Carl Friedrich Goerdeler, the former mayor of Leipzig and one of the leaders of German resistance to Hitler, appears at the People's Court, having been arrested after the failed coup in August 1944. Found guilty, he was kept alive because he continued to name names in an effort to show the Nazis the extent of the resistance. He was hanged in February 1945. (Topfoto)

speak with a single voice against Hitler. Indeed, at the outset it actually welcomed the Nazi experiment, which seemed to espouse Christian values. Even before coming to power, the Nazis had looked to absorb the Protestant Church into the movement with the establishment of the Deutsche Christen (German Christians). Following the Nazi accession to power on 30 January 1933, this group sought to control the Protestant Church with some success, but ultimately the Deutsche Christen splintered and differences between it and the mainstream Church diminished to such an extent that, in the end, it was treated no differently by Germany's Nazi government.

Having failed to absorb the Protestant Church, the Nazis moved from a policy of grudging acceptance to outright opposition and, in 1941, called for the Church to be eliminated completely. Church leaders continued to protest against Nazism, but this stand could not be described as political resistance; rather, it was a fight to preserve the autonomy of the Protestant Church. This reluctance to move into the political arena was the result of a number of factors, not the least of which was the problem of Church versus State – to attack the Nazis was to attack Germany. This was particularly true following the outbreak of war, as the Church put patriotic duty above attempts to attack the regime. Moreover, the fight against Bolshevism proved a persuasive argument for both Protestants and Catholics, neutralizing much of the opposition against the Nazis.

The position of the Catholic Church was different from that of the Protestants because of the extra-national dimension of the Church of Rome. On 20 July 1933 the Vatican signed a concordat with Germany recognizing the Nazi regime, which made opposition to the Nazis difficult. As such, the Catholic Church never sanctioned political resistance, but individuals – both Protestant and Catholic – did demur and played a part in the plot of 20 July, and the Nazis continued to fear the power of the Church.

The pastor and theologian Martin Niemöller neatly captured the state of German opposition in Germany at that time when he wrote:

Bendlerstrasse, now Stauffenbergstrasse, where the Bendlerblock was located. This was the location of the headquarters of the Replacement Army. It is still used by the German Ministry of Defence and is also home to the German Resistance Memorial Centre. Just visible in the bottom right is the entrance to the courtyard where von Stauffenberg and his compatriots were executed. (Author)

When the Nazis came for the Communists
I was silent
I wasn't a Communist
When the Nazis came for the Social Democrats
I was silent
I wasn't a Social Democrat
When the Nazis came for the Trade Unionists
I was silent
I wasn't a Trade Unionist
When the Nazis came for the Jews
I was silent
I wasn't a Jew
When the Nazis came for me
There was no one left to Protest (quoted in McDonough 2001: 38)

Neither the political Left nor the Church were able to challenge the Nazis and, while there was opposition to Hitler and the Nazis from other quarters, including the civil service and academia, it was never possible to unite the various groups into a single movement. Only one group could realistically remove Hitler from power, and that was the army. However, at the outset this powerful body, by adopting a neutral stance, served to consolidate Nazi rule. Promised autonomy by Hitler, the army acquiesced in the murder of Kurt von Schleicher, a former general and the last Chancellor of the Weimar Republic, in the Night of the Long Knives and, following the death of President Hindenburg on 2 August 1934, accepted an oath swearing allegiance to Hitler. Moreover, it could be argued, initially at least, that the aims of the army and the Nazis were broadly aligned, both parties sharing a desire to overturn the punitive peace agreed at Versailles and to expand the armed forces.

The German military and Hitler

In the pre-war period, then, the army was content to carry out its duty and not get involved in politics. Opposition was generally confined to the conscience of individuals, rather than any coordinated action by the army as a whole. The Army High Command (known as the Oberkommando des Heeres – OKH – from 1936) did depart momentarily from this course as Hitler's expansionist aims became clear. In 1936, in contravention of the terms of the peace agreed at Versailles, Hitler planned to remilitarize the Rhineland. Generaloberst Ludwig Beck, Generalstabschef des Heeres (Chief of the Army General Staff), implored his superiors – Generalfeldmarschall Werner von Blomberg, Reichskriegsminister (Minister of Defence) and also Oberbefehlshaber der Wehrmacht (Supreme Commander of the Armed Forces) and Generaloberst Werner Freiherr von Fritsch, Oberbefehlshaber des Heeres (Army Commander-in-Chief) – to act, but they did nothing.[1] The following year Blomberg and Fritsch attended the Hossbach conference (5 November 1937), where Hitler outlined his policy of *Lebensraum* (living space). Both commanders were shocked, but within months they had been replaced, their positions undermined by personal intrigues.

At the same time Hitler used this crisis to strengthen his hold over the military. All members of the Wehrmacht were already required to make a personal oath of loyalty to the Führer. In February 1938 Hitler established the Oberkommando der Wehrmacht (OKW – High Command of the German Armed Forces) and made himself Oberster Befehlshaber (Supreme Commander), with General der Artillerie (General of Artillery), later Generalfeldmarschall, Wilhelm Keitel appointed as OKW chief of staff.

The army, though, still had a powerful voice, and Beck continued to press Fritsch's replacement, Generalfeldmarschall Walther von Brauchitsch, to act. Though sympathetic, Brauchitsch did nothing to influence Hitler and, with the Western powers seemingly unwilling to take action, Beck resigned in

---

1 The Reichswehr (German Armed Forces), created after World War I, became the Wehrmacht in 1935; the Reichsheer (German Army) was renamed the Heer.

SEPTEMBER 1938

Beck abandons planned *coup d'état* after the signing of the Munich Agreement

8 NOVEMBER 1939

Johann Georg Elser's attempt to kill Hitler at the Munich Beer Hall fails

19 DECEMBER 1941

Hitler becomes Oberbefehlshaber des Heeres

August 1938. A close associate of Beck's, Generalmajor Hans Oster, continued to plot against the Nazis. Working in the central department (Abteilung Z) of the Abwehr (military intelligence), he had many contacts and was protected by Konteradmiral Wilhelm Canaris, the head of the Abwehr. In the summer of 1938 plans were hatched to arrest Hitler following the outbreak of war in Europe, which now seemed inevitable. His incarceration would be followed by the establishment of a military junta until power could be passed back to a democratic government. Contacts were made with the Western powers to apprise them of the plan, but the conspirators were ignored and, on 30 September 1938, the Munich Peace Agreement was signed, which effectively cut the ground from beneath the conspirators.

The coming of war

The German invasion of Poland on 1 September 1939 and the outbreak of war changed the complexion of resistance to Hitler. The army grew in size and strength and was therefore in many respects better placed to oppose the Nazi regime. However, the expansion of the army, the creation of the Luftwaffe and especially the growth of the Waffen-SS (Armed SS), the military wing of the Nazis' Schutzstaffel (protection squad), saw the ranks of the armed forces swollen with Nazis, which served to undermine the strength of the officer class – the mainstay of the resistance. Moreover, the war also made resistance to Hitler more difficult because it blurred the edges between Germany and the Nazi government. It would be difficult to attack Hitler without possible criticism of stabbing the country in the back. This was a powerful charge, because it resonated with the stab-in-the-back theory expounded after World War I. In 1918 politicians had signed an armistice when, it was argued, the German Army had not been defeated in the field. Significantly, it was also difficult to act against Hitler while he was enjoying success. On 1 September 1939 Germany invaded Poland and, in a little over a month, Hitler's military, in conjunction with Soviet forces, proved victorious.

With the defeat of Poland, Hitler's gaze turned west and plans were developed for the invasion of France, which was scheduled for October 1939. The army, nervous about the prospect of another European war with France and Britain, expressed deep misgivings and the attack was delayed. In the interval further attempts were made to win over Western governments. This showed signs of success and Britain and France guaranteed friendly relations with a non-Nazi Germany, provided that all expansionist plans were renounced. However, despite knowing about this deal, Brauchitsch failed to act once again and, in April 1940, Germany occupied Denmark and Norway. Peace talks with the Western powers ended and this seeming duplicity generated a mistrust of the German military that lasted until the end of the war.[2]

The invasion of France and the Low Countries – about which Oster warned the West[3] – was launched on 10 May 1940; within weeks the British

2   In Britain and France some felt that the peace overtures by the army were a ruse to enable the Germans to attack Scandinavia.
3   He provided the dates of the planned attack.

had evacuated the Continent and France had surrendered, leaving the opposition with little or no hope of help from the outside. Change would have to come from within, but chances were slim. Any act against Hitler would be seen as treason. Moreover, for those officers who had conspired to remove Hitler because his actions threatened to destroy Germany and all they held dear was to some extent pacified by the victories. Plans to overthrow Hitler continued, but, with little support inside or outside the country, the movement was fuelled only by the belief among conspirators that they were morally right.

On 22 June 1941 Germany invaded the Soviet Union. Just like it had in the West the Wehrmacht won a series of startling victories, but it soon became clear that war on the Eastern Front was going to be different, not least because of the brutal way Hitler was waging war. The people of the occupied territories, whom the Nazis viewed as *Untermenschen* (subhumans), were systematically abused – particularly the Jews, who were rounded up and shot or sent to concentration camps. Hitler was also increasingly involved in directing military operations, which worried many in the army. In the bitter winter of 1941/42 Hitler insisted that his exhausted forces capture Moscow and, when Generaloberst Erich Hoepner, who had formed part of the conspiracy to remove Hitler before the war, dared to defy Hitler's orders by withdrawing troops of his Panzergruppe 4 (4th Armoured Group), he was removed from his command. Hoepner did not forget this humiliation and it strengthened his conviction that Hitler should be removed. A number of other senior officers were also dismissed or asked to be relieved of their command and, on 19 December 1941, Hitler made himself Army Commander-in-Chief, vice Brauchitsch. In 1942 the Wehrmacht resumed its offensive on the Eastern Front, but now Hitler changed the focus of the attack with the main effort in the south. On 28 June, Fall Blau (Case Blue) was launched and in September the first German troops entered Stalingrad. Hitler was determined to capture the city and Stalin was equally determined it would not fall. In November the Soviet leader launched a counter-attack, which saw Generalfeldmarschall Friedrich Paulus's 6. Armee (Sixth Army) encircled in the city and steadily annihilated; Paulus surrendered on 31 January 1943. Many in the army were now convinced that the only way to save Germany was to remove Hitler from power.

INITIAL STRATEGY

Failures and frustrations

Resistance in the army initially coalesced around Oberst (later Generalmajor) Henning von Tresckow, who was Chief of Operations, Heeresgruppe Mitte (Army Group Centre). He tried to persuade the new commander of Army Group Centre, Generalfeldmarschall Günther von Kluge, to join the conspiracy, but Kluge was ambivalent. Indeed, in October 1942, Kluge accepted a large payment from the Führer for his good conduct, which made it difficult for him to act against his benefactor. But if Kluge would not act, others would. Already in February 1943 a number of senior officers in Heeresgruppe B (Army Group B) planned to arrest Hitler when he visited Poltava in the Ukraine.[4] It was recognized that there would be resistance from his security personnel and, as such, the conspirators were prepared, if necessary, to kill Hitler then and there. However, instead of flying to Poltava as planned, Hitler flew to Saporoshe and the plan was scrapped.

The difficulties of arresting and killing Hitler were now very apparent and it was understood that a more effective method of removing him was needed. The conspirators hit on the idea of planting a bomb on Hitler's aircraft and detonating it while he was airborne. This would not only kill their nemesis but had the added benefit of potentially deflecting blame away from the army. A plan was developed and, on 13 March 1943, two British Clam mines disguised as a Cointreau bottle were smuggled onto Hitler's plane by Oberleutnant Fabian von Schlabrendorff, one of Tresckow's co-conspirators. The detonator was activated, but the device did not go off. Hitler landed safely and the conspirators had to recover the bomb. Seemingly the extreme cold in the hold meant that the detonator did not activate the explosives. The so-called *Smolensk Attentat* (attempted assassination) had failed.

---

4 Heeresgruppe Süd (Army Group South) was split into two army groups: A and B.

A week later, on 21 March, a further opportunity presented itself at the *Heldengedenktag* (Heroes' Memorial Day) in Berlin. Oberst Rudolf-Christoph Freiherr von Gersdorff of the staff of Army Group Centre planned to plant a bomb in the hall where Hitler was due to give a speech. He reconnoitred the room, but security was tight (following Johann Georg Elser's unsuccessful attempt in Munich on 8 November 1939) and there was no opportunity to hide the bomb, let alone get to it again to prime the detonator. Recognizing that this approach was not feasible, Gersdorff now considered an alternative. He would strap explosives to himself and detonate them after Hitler's speech when he visited the exhibition of captured equipment. For this he ideally needed an instantaneous fuse, but none could be sourced in the time available, so he used a timed fuse. Hitler completed his speech and headed for the exhibition. Gersdorff set the timer running, but Hitler fairly galloped through the exhibits and was gone. The assassin could only remove the timer and deposit it down the toilet before the explosives were detonated.

MAY 1942
First meeting of the Kreisau Circle

In the first half of 1943 four failed attempts had been made on Hitler's life. But if the conspirators were depressed about their lack of success they were equally perturbed by the parlous state of the war by late 1943. The Wehrmacht had suffered defeats in North Africa and, significantly, at Stalingrad, and Italy signed an armistice with the Western Allies in September 1943. Importantly, in January 1943 the Allies met at Casablanca and agreed a policy of unconditional surrender. Kluge, Generalfeldmarschall Georg von Küchler, the commander of Heeresgruppe Nord (Army Group North), and Generalfeldmarschall Erich von Manstein, commander of Heeresgruppe Süd (Army Group South), now signalled their support for action, but it only extended as far as representations to Hitler to end the war. However, nothing was done and, in October 1943, Kluge was injured in a car crash; this potential figurehead for the resistance was thereby removed from the equation – at least in the short term.

In spite of this setback a further unsuccessful attempt on Hitler's life was made in December 1943. Hauptmann Axel Freiherr von dem Bussche-Streithorst, one of Tresckow's co-conspirators, again planned a suicide attack using a bomb with a hand-grenade fuse to detonate it. Hitler was due to attend an exhibition of uniforms and military equipment and, while he was there, Bussche would embrace the Führer and kill them both. However, the exhibition was postponed and Bussche had to return to the front. Another officer offered to take his place when the exhibition was rearranged but again the show was postponed.

Finally, on 11 March 1944, Rittmeister Eberhard von Breitenbuch, aide-de-camp to Generalfeldmarschall Ernst Busch, the new commander of Army Group Centre, came to the Berghof, the Führer's residence near Berchtesgaden in the Bavarian Alps, on the pretext of briefing Hitler, but secretly planning to shoot him dead. Armed with a pistol he prepared to meet the Führer, but was refused entry and the attempt was cancelled.

13 MARCH 1943
Bomb secreted on Hitler's aircraft fails to explode

The failure of the various assassination attempts coincided with a series of setbacks for the resistance. Firstly, the Abwehr, so long a haven for resistance, was dissolved. In 1943 the Gestapo raided Oster's department

Claus Schenk Graf von Stauffenberg with co-conspirator Albrecht Ritter Mertz von Quirnheim (on the right). The photograph was taken in the summer of 1942 at OKH headquarters in Vinnitsa, in the Ukraine. Two years later they were again side by side in the courtyard of the Bendlerblock facing a firing squad. (Topfoto)

and he was dismissed from his post that April; in February 1944 Canaris was also dismissed and the Abwehr was merged with the Sicherheitsdienst (the SS Intelligence agency). Secondly, the leader of the so-called Kreisau Circle,[5] Helmuth James Graf von Moltke, was arrested by the Gestapo in January 1944 along with a number of other members, thus eliminating another centre of resistance.

Also in April 1943, one of the most able and determined members of the resistance was severely injured while serving in North Africa. Claus Schenk Graf von Stauffenberg was wounded in an air attack; he lost his left eye, his right hand was amputated above the wrist and he lost the ring and little fingers on his left. In spite of this, Stauffenberg's desire to assassinate Hitler was undimmed, but to Stauffenberg's co-conspirators his handicaps were considered so severe that he could not possibly be considered to carry out the assassination of Hitler. Moreover, after any attempt on Hitler's life, Stauffenberg's skills would be needed in Berlin to direct the coup. In the summer of 1943 the debate was academic at any rate, because Stauffenberg had no access to the Führer.

New opportunities

This changed first in November 1943, when Stauffenberg was made chief of staff to General der Infanterie (General of Infantry) Friedrich Olbricht, chief of the *Allgemeines Heeresamt* (General Army Office), and then in June 1944, when he was made chief of staff to Generaloberst Friedrich Fromm, the commander-in-chief of the Replacement Army. Ironically, the decision to appoint Stauffenberg was made by Hitler's chief adjutant, Generalleutnant Rudolf Schmundt, one of the Führer's most trusted advisors, who would be seriously injured by the bomb explosion on 20 July.

Almost immediately upon taking up his post, Stauffenberg explained to Fromm his intention to kill Hitler. Fromm greeted the news with indifference and neither the conversation nor Stauffenberg's plan were ever mentioned again. With no explicit direction from his superior to abandon the idea, Stauffenberg continued with his preparations. British-made explosives, more powerful than anything produced in Germany, were sourced by Army Group Centre and were sent by courier to East Prussia, where they were secreted at Mauerwald, the location of OKH headquarters near to the Wolfsschanze. Normally, this would have been the ideal location, but because of building work, Hitler and his support staff were temporarily located at Berchtesgaden.

---

5   This group of German dissidents was centred on the Kreisau estate of Helmuth James Graf von Moltke.

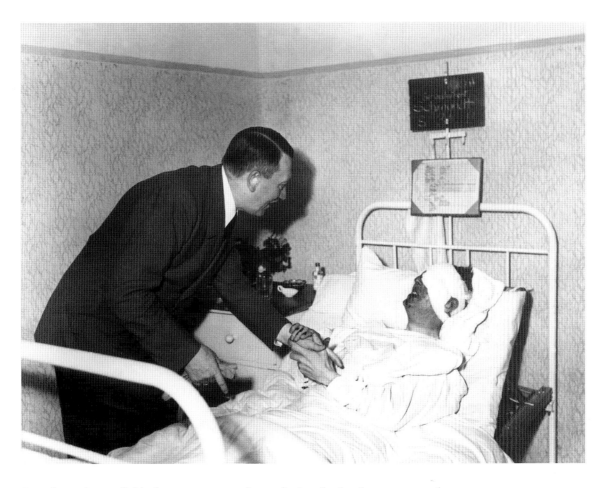

In order to be available for any attempt the explosives had to be transported by train to Berlin, where they were delivered to Stauffenberg on 25 May. He now had the tools; he just needed the opportunity to use them.

At the end of May Stauffenberg made his first trip to Berchtesgaden in preparation for a briefing to the Führer at the beginning of June. It is unclear if he believed that this first meeting would provide an opportunity to put his plan into action, not least because Oberst Albrecht Ritter Mertz von Quirnheim, the man who had replaced Stauffenberg as Olbricht's chief of staff and who would lead the coup in Berlin, was still on leave. Even so, fate intervened once again and, on 6 June 1944, the Western Allies landed in Normandy. Stauffenberg was now caught on the horns of a dilemma; with Germany fighting on two fronts, the end of the war was surely imminent and he therefore questioned whether there was any point in assassinating Hitler. Through an intermediary he asked Tresckow, who was still a leading light in the conspiracy despite his geographic separation, what he should do. Tresckow was categorical in his response: 'The assassination of Hitler must take place ... Even if it does not succeed, the *coup d'état* must be attempted. The point now is not the practical purpose, but to prove to the world and before history that the German resistance have staked their all and put their lives on the line...' (quoted in Hoffmann 2008: 238).

Hitler visits Generalleutnant Rudolf Schmundt in hospital near the Wolfsschanze following the blast on 20 July. Schmundt was head of the Heerespersonalamt and initially made a good recovery, but died in October from complications arising from injuries suffered in the explosion. (Topfoto)

**NOVEMBER
1943**

**Stauffenberg
appointed
Olbricht's chief of
staff**

**20 JUNE
1944**

**Stauffenberg
appointed Fromm's
chief of staff**

His faith restored, Stauffenberg once again returned to his plans. These had to be matured quickly, as events in Germany and at the front were making an early strike imperative. Dr Julius Leber and Dr Adolf Reichwein, Socialist leaders who were close to Stauffenberg, had been arrested at the beginning of July along with a number of Communist leaders with whom they had met. By this time the Allies had consolidated their foothold in Normandy and the Soviets had launched their summer offensive on the Eastern Front on 22 June; in less than three weeks the Red Army had smashed through Army Group Centre, with 28 German divisions destroyed or captured.

Hitler, flanked by Stauffenberg (left), Puttkamer and Keitel (right), greets General der Flieger Karl-Heinrich Bodenschatz in front of the guest bunker at the Wolfsschanze on 15 July 1944. Of interest are the fake trees, which helped camouflage the headquarters from aerial observation. (Topfoto)

While the need to expedite any assassination plans was clear, the conspirators had to consider the potential fallout of any assassination attempt. Following Hitler's death, who would be the natural successor? Would he be able to muster enough support to threaten or crush the coup? Reichsmarschall Hermann Göring had fallen from favour, but he was still the anointed successor to Hitler. He was head of the Luftwaffe, which had flourished under the Nazis and was unquestionably the most loyal of the three services. Reichsführer-SS Heinrich Himmler was another potential leader. He commanded the SS and, as such, was a powerful figure. The conspirators therefore agreed that Hitler, Göring and Himmler should be killed at the same time. This was logical, but impractical. Göring rarely turned up to military briefings and although Himmler did, his attendance was patchy. The consequences of this decision were soon to become apparent. Up to this point Stauffenberg believed that Generalmajor Helmuth Stieff would plant the explosives. He was a member of the resistance and, as head of the Organizational Section at OKH, he was in regular contact with the Führer.

On 7 July Stieff had an ideal opportunity to plant a bomb when, after much persuasion, Hitler agreed to attend a uniform and equipment exhibition at Klessheim, near Salzburg (the show that had been postponed from December 1943), but Stieff called off the attempt. The reason is unclear; he may have lost his nerve, or it may have been because Göring and Himmler were not present. Certainly this latter factor was the reason for the cancellation of the 11 July attempt. On this occasion Stauffenberg was due to be at Hitler's briefing in the afternoon at the Berghof. However, in the morning Stauffenberg learned that the respective heads of the Luftwaffe and the SS would not be in attendance. Stieff hesitated once again and directed Stauffenberg to postpone the attempt, much to Stauffenberg's displeasure. This proved to be the last opportunity at the Berghof. Three days later Hitler moved his headquarters back to the Wolfsschanze, even though the building work was incomplete. Any attempt on Hitler's life would now have to be carried out at the Wolfsschanze.

THE PLAN

A difficult target

The previous attempts by the military to kill Hitler had typically been perpetrated when he was on his travels and was consequently more vulnerable to attack. However, the secrecy surrounding Hitler's movements and his tendency to alter his schedule at the last minute made planning an attack problematic. This not only meant it was difficult to predict with any certainty that he would be killed, but also that it would be extremely difficult to set in motion any plan to seize power once he was dead. In this respect, it would be easier to target the Führer when he was at one of his private residences or specially constructed headquarters. However, this was challenging for different reasons, not the least of which was gaining access and then getting close enough to Hitler to carry out the attack without being stopped by security.

Before the war Hitler divided his time between the German capital, Berlin, his spiritual home, Munich, and his specially constructed mountain residence, the Berghof, near Berchtesgaden in the Bavarian Alps. With the outbreak of war he was keen to stay close to the front and, during the Polish campaign, he travelled on a specially adapted train. However, it was apparent that this was a far from perfect solution. For the invasion of France and the Low Countries a number of specially constructed *Führerhauptquartiere* (FHQ – Führer headquarters) were built near Germany's western border, from where Hitler could oversee operations. When Fall Gelb (Case Yellow) was launched in May 1940 Hitler stayed at FHQ Felsennest, a set of converted Westwall bunkers near Bad Münstereifel. As the German forces advanced, a further headquarters was built in the small village of Brûly-de-Pesche in Belgium, which was known as FHQ Wolfsschlucht. Stays in these FHQs were generally short and reflected the relative ease with which the German forces overcame the opposition.

The same was expected in the east when Hitler launched Fall Barbarossa, the Axis invasion of the Soviet Union, in June 1941. Along the border three rudimentary headquarters were constructed in East Prussia and occupied Poland. The most important of these was FHQ Wolfsschanze (Wolf's Lair). This was built in the Görlitz Forest in East Prussia and straddled the road and railway line between Rastenburg (now Kętrzyn in Poland) and Angerburg (now Węgorzewo, also in Poland). Work had begun on the site in 1940 and consisted of a series of concrete and brick hutments to accommodate Hitler and his personal staff, along with a mess, communication centre, garage and a heating plant.

With the failure of the German forces to capture Moscow in December 1941, it was clear that the war would continue for some time and, during the following year, improvements were made to the Wolfsschanze so that it was more suited to its role as a military headquarters. Finally, in February 1944, with the war still dragging on, a further (and final) building phase began that saw the construction of a number of new bunkers and the massive strengthening of existing buildings, including the Führerbunker. Hitler had always had an interest in concrete fortifications and had developed the design for the new bunker himself. He envisaged the existing structure being encased in concrete 3m thick with a further concrete jacket around this, some 5m thick, and in between the two a layer of sand that would serve to absorb any bomb blast. Speer described the finished building as 'an ancient Egyptian tomb. It was actually nothing but a great windowless block of concrete, without direct ventilation, in cross section a building whose masses of concrete far exceeded the usable cubic feet of space' (Speer 1970: 526).

Surrounding the Führerbunker and those of Bormann, Göring and Keitel was a barbed-wire fence with two entrances, one to the west and one to the east. This enclave was known as Sperrkreis I (Security Zone I). In September 1943 security within Sperrkreis I was increased with the establishment of Sperrkreis A. An additional fence was erected around the Führerbunker and the buildings in the immediate vicinity. Later, when the Führerbunker was being strengthened, a similar security zone was established around the *Luftschutzraum für Gäste* (guest bunker), where Hitler resided temporarily, and an adjacent building – the *Lagebaracke* (briefing hut). It was here that Hitler held his briefing on 20 July. Sperrkreis I was located at the eastern end of FHQ Wolfsschanze. Surrounding the whole complex (which was known as Sperrkreis II) was a fence, punctuated by guard towers and three entrances located to the west, east and south of the site. The last of these linked the headquarters with the airfield at Rastenburg. The perimeter was further reinforced with minefields, blockhouses and machine-gun posts, along with anti-aircraft positions to guard against air attack. Further afield, checkpoints were established on roads and at junctions.

Hitler's personal security

The job of guarding the site against commando and paratrooper attacks was the responsibility of the army's Führer-Begleit-Bataillon (FBB – Führer Escort Battalion). These men were recruited from Infanterie-Regiment

CLAUS SCHENK GRAF VON STAUFFENBERG

Claus Schenk Graf von Stauffenberg was born in Jettingen in Swabia on 15 November 1907. His father was in the service of the Württemberg royal family and his mother was a descendant of Gneisenau, the famous Prussian general. He was educated at the Eberhard Ludwig Grammar School along with his older twin brothers, Alexander and Berthold. Brought up in the Catholic faith, the brothers were imbued with a sense of duty towards society. Though deeply imbued with the Christian principles of Catholicism, Claus and his brothers also became admirers of the poet Stefan George, who had a decisive influence on their political and philosophical thinking.[1]

Upon leaving school, Stauffenberg joined the army as a cavalryman in 1926. In 1930, after passing his officers' examination, he was made a Leutnant and posted to Bamberg, north of Nuremberg. The ensuing period proved to be a significant time of change in his life, both domestically and politically. In November 1930 he became engaged to Nina Freiin von Lerchenfeld and they were married in 1933. They had three sons and two daughters – the last, Constanze, was born in 1945 after Stauffenberg's death. Politically, Germany was experiencing an extraordinary change and, at that time, Stauffenberg expressed his admiration for Hitler and saw National Socialism as a force for good. In January 1933 he welcomed the appointment of Adolf Hitler as chancellor.

At the outbreak of the war he was serving with 6. Panzer-Division; he fought in Poland in 1939 and in France in 1940. At this time he was still a supporter of the regime and even turned down a request to join the resistance. However, by 1942 he had changed his mind and openly expressed his dislike of Hitler and the Nazis, particularly the treatment of the Jews and the population of occupied territories. Stauffenberg was by now convinced that Hitler had to be assassinated.

In February 1943 he was posted to North Africa as an Oberstleutnant, before being severely wounded in an air attack in April. He was evacuated and began his recuperation in Munich. Stauffenberg was deemed unfit for front-line service and General der Infanterie Olbricht requested he become his chief of staff. Together they adapted the *Valkyrie* plans for suppressing civil disturbances as a vehicle for overthrowing the Nazis. Stauffenberg also strove to develop contacts with other resistance groups. As Fromm's chief of staff from June 1944, Stauffenberg had access to Hitler's briefings and decided to use the opportunity this afforded him to kill Hitler.

A portrait of Claus Schenk Graf von Stauffenberg. A strong critic of the Nazis, he was injured in 1943 in North Africa and was later posted to the Replacement Army where he had access to the Führer. This he used to devastating effect on 20 July 1944 when he planted the bomb designed to kill Hitler. (Topfoto)

1   Stefan George was a poet and thinker who advocated a new order led by intellectual or artistic elites. Stauffenberg often quoted George's poetry, especially after the latter's death in 1933. George's poetry was admired by many National Socialists, but George kept aloof from politics.

'Grossdeutschland' and were extremely well trained and equipped with modern weapons – befitting a unit given such an important task. While the FBB was responsible for external security, the Reichssicherheitsdienst (RSD – Reich Security Service) was responsible for internal security. It was split into a series of agencies, with Dienststelle 1 (Bureau 1) specifically responsible for the Führer's security. Most members of the RSD were former police officers, which reflected the nature of their work, gathering intelligence on possible threats and checking routes and venues that Hitler would use. RSD officers were also responsible for vetting workers involved in the construction of Hitler's headquarters. They were given SS ranks and uniforms but, unusually, they were commanded by Hitler rather than Himmler, the Reichsführer-SS.

Hitler's personal security was the responsibility of the SS-Begleit-Kommando (SS Escort Detachment) – not to be confused with the FBB. These men were drawn from the SS and, more specifically, the SS-Leibstandarte (SS Body Guard Regiment). Only 30 or so men were allocated to protect Hitler (which included day-to-day duties such as preparing his clothes and taking him messages), but more than 100 more were employed at Hitler's other residences and headquarters.[6]

The security around Hitler was, therefore, extremely tight, and it would not be feasible for the conspirators to attempt a 'normal' raid with any genuine hope of success. Instead, the conspirators would, as they had tried previously, seek to attend a meeting with the Führer, plant a bomb and then leave. The physical dangers of such a plan were considerably less than those posed by a *coup de main*, but it would still take an enormous amount of courage.

The conspirators

The man who would carry out the attack was Oberst Claus Schenk Graf von Stauffenberg. He had already been involved in one aborted attempt on Hitler's life, but he was now determined to succeed and was joined in this endeavour by other members of his wider family. These included his brother Berthold, his cousin Oberstleutnant Cäsar von Hofacker, who would liaise between the conspirators in Paris and Berlin, and another cousin, Peter Yorck Graf von Wartenburg, who was a member of the Kreisau Circle.

In Berlin the coup would be implemented by General der Infanterie Friedrich Olbricht. Olbricht was born in 1888 and served in World War I, during which time he was decorated for bravery. A career soldier, he fought in the 1939 Polish campaign and was again decorated for bravery. In 1940 he was appointed head of the General Army Office at OKH in Berlin. From 1942 he was responsible for developing the Operation *Valkyrie* plans for managing civil unrest. Olbricht's chief of staff, whom he appointed, was a like-minded soldier, Oberst Albrecht Ritter Mertz von Quirnheim. Born in Munich in 1905, he joined the Reichswehr and made steady progress through the ranks until, in 1944, he was made Oberst and succeeded

---

6   To confuse matters still further, when Hitler was on trips equal numbers of RSD and SS-Begleit-Kommando staff accompanied him; this combined unit was known as the Führer-Begleit-Kommando, though both groups fiercely maintained their independence.

Generalmajor Henning von Tresckow was chief of staff at Army Group Centre. He was vehemently anti-Nazi and gathered like-minded officers around him, and tried on a number of occasions to kill Hitler. On hearing of Stauffenberg's failed attempt, he killed himself. (Topfoto)

Stauffenberg as chief of staff to Olbricht. Mertz von Quirnheim had known Stauffenberg since 1925 and they had served together on the Eastern Front. As a young man Mertz von Quirnheim had also got to know Oberleutnant Werner von Haeften and his brother. Haeften was born in Berlin in 1908 and joined the army at the outbreak of World War II. He was badly wounded while serving on the Eastern Front and, after convalescing, was posted as Stauffenberg's adjutant on the staff of the commander of the Replacement Army.

Following Hitler's assassination, Generaloberst Ludwig Beck was to become Head of State. He was born in 1880 and was Chef der Truppenamt (Chief of the Troop Office) from 1933 to 1935 and then Chief of the Army General Staff from 1935 to 1938. Along with Generalleutnant Carl-Heinrich von Stülpnagel (who, as a General der Infanterie, was to lead the coup in Paris), Beck had sought to overthrow Hitler prior to the outbreak of war. Following Beck's resignation on 18 August 1938 he became a focal point for military opposition to Hitler and, during the war, he became a central figure in the resistance.

Generalmajor Henning von Tresckow, who had served under Beck, was born in 1901 in Magdeburg and came from a family with a strong military tradition. He served in World War I and remained in the armed forces before leaving in 1920 to look after the family estate. In 1934 he rejoined the army and, after the invasion of the Soviet Union, served on the Eastern Front. In his senior position he was able to recruit like-minded individuals into key positions in Army Group Centre so that they could attempt to kill Hitler, though none of the attempts were successful. He helped Olbricht to adapt the Operation *Valkyrie* plans, but was unable to help in their implementation because of his duties on the Eastern Front.

The plan takes shape

The plan to kill Hitler was thus relatively simple. Under the auspices of providing a briefing to the Führer, Stauffenberg would plant a bomb that would be detonated by a simple timer. Having positioned the bomb, he would make his excuse to leave the building and then escape from the base in the confusion that followed the blast. However, if the mechanics of the assassination were straightforward, the plan to seize power afterwards was anything but. Even with Hitler dead the Nazi power structure would still be in place and one of Hitler's acolytes would undoubtedly fill the vacuum. To prevent this from happening the Nazi machine had to be destroyed, or at least usurped. The mechanism for doing this was already in place.

Within Germany there existed a very real threat of internal unrest, either as a result of civil disturbances brought on by the privations of war and the incessant bombing, or as a possible insurrection by the millions of foreign forced labourers working in the country. In order to cope with either eventuality a plan was developed, Operation *Valkyrie*, which would see executive power and military leadership being entrusted to the commander of the Replacement Army. Very early on, Olbricht had recognized the potential for using such a plan in the overthrow of Hitler. He was responsible for maintaining these emergency powers and *Valkyrie* was adapted on a number of occasions to suit the needs of the conspiracy; effectively, it became a blueprint for a *coup d'état*. Once Hitler had been assassinated the conspirators would use the *Valkyrie* orders to take control of the key government, party and Wehrmacht offices in Berlin and in the wider Reich. Previously identified senior members of the resistance would then take up key government posts and negotiations would be started with the Allies to agree a peace deal. Once stability had been achieved there would be a transition to a democratically elected government. This was the plan that Stauffenberg and his co-conspirators would use to kill Hitler and seize power.

THE RAID

15 July: a missed opportunity

On 15 July Fromm and Stauffenberg were ordered to travel to the Wolfsschanze to attend a series of briefings with Hitler; at one of these Stauffenberg planned to detonate his bomb. In Berlin, Mertz von Quirnheim placed the troops in the city on alert for Operation *Valkyrie*. This was done at 1100hrs, about the same time that Stauffenberg left for Rastenburg – a full six hours ahead of any assassination attempt. This suggests that Mertz von Quirnheim and Stauffenberg had already decided that Hitler must die, irrespective of whether Himmler and Göring were present at Hitler's briefing. However, this conviction was not shared by the other conspirators. They were insistent that as a bare minimum Himmler must also perish in any explosion. That this view was not impressed on Stauffenberg before he departed is baffling, but when he arrived Stieff relayed the message to him and, when it was clear that only Hitler would be present, Stieff aborted the operation. Stauffenberg was understandably perplexed and angry, and adding to his indignation was the fact that he knew that troops in and around Berlin had been placed on alert to march into the government quarter and seize key sites once the *Valkyrie* order was issued.

Showing admirable composure Stauffenberg attended the various briefings but excused himself on two occasions to make calls to his co-conspirators. He pressed them to reconsider their thinking that both Göring and Himmler had to die at the same time and to seize the opportunity, but they were not for turning. Frustrated, he called Mertz von Quirnheim and they decided to act unilaterally, but by this time the briefings had concluded and the chance was gone. The units that had been put on alert were stood down and told it was simply an exercise. However, when Fromm heard about what had happened he reprimanded Olbricht; no such liberties could be taken in the future. Mobilization could now only happen after the attempt on Hitler's life, which introduced a delay into the plan that would prove critical on 20 July.

When Stauffenberg arrived back in Berlin he held a post-mortem. Mertz von Quirnheim provided a gloomy appraisal of the conspirators in the Bendlerblock, who, he believed, lacked the courage to see the exercise through to its conclusion. Indeed, it seemed that they were greatly relieved to learn that the assassination attempt had been called off. Dispirited, but not deterred, the pair agreed to kill Hitler come what may, and time was now of the essence. On 17 July news reached them that a warrant for the arrest of Carl Friedrich Goerdeler, former Lord Mayor of Leipzig and for so long the leader of the civilian resistance, had been issued. More worryingly, they later learned of the rumours circulating in Berlin that some kind of attack was to be perpetrated at the Wolfsschanze in the near future. Stauffenberg decided he had to strike now, whether Göring and Himmler would be killed at the same time or not. Hitler had to be eliminated and he would be the man to do it. In so doing he was prepared to renounce his oath of allegiance and accept the almost certain charge of treason and the penalty that went with it.

20 JULY 1944
0700hrs

Stauffenberg and Haeften depart from Rangsdorf

While working as Fromm's chief of staff, Stauffenberg lived with his family in a house on the Tristranstrasse. Stauffenberg travelled from here to Rangsdorf airport in Berlin, from where he flew to the Wolfsschanze and planted the bomb. (Topfoto)

To the Wolfsschanze

On 18 July Stauffenberg received orders to head to the Wolfsschanze on the 20th to brief Hitler; he was to provide details of plans for the establishment of two new divisions to defend East Prussia. The day he received his orders coincided with the departure of his wife and family to Lautlingen, south of Stuttgart, for their summer vacation. Stauffenberg asked his wife Nina to delay their departure, but the tickets had been bought and so they duly set off. On 19 July Stauffenberg tried to call his wife but he was unable to get through because of an Allied air raid. The next morning he was due to fly to the Wolfsschanze with the explosives to assassinate Hitler.

On the morning of 20 July Gefreiter (Lance-Corporal) Karl Schweizer drove Stauffenberg to Rangsdorf Airfield to take the regular courier flight to the Wolfsschanze. Haeften, Stauffenberg's aide-de-camp, met him at the airfield and the two boarded the flight. Schweizer set the briefcase containing the explosives next to Stauffenberg. As they prepared to leave Schweizer was directed to collect Stauffenberg and Haeften from the airfield that afternoon.

The plane landed at Rastenburg shortly after 1000hrs and Stauffenberg was taken to the Wolfsschanze, where he had breakfast with members of the Camp Commandant's staff, including Hauptmann Heinz Pieper, a staff officer who arranged Stauffenberg's car, and Rittmeister Leonhard von Möllendorff, a personnel officer. Meanwhile Haeften and Stieff, who had joined Stauffenberg on the flight, headed to Mauerwald with the explosives. After breakfast Stauffenberg had to attend a series of briefings, the last of which was at 1130hrs with Generalfeldmarschall Keitel. Although not invited to this meeting, Haeften returned to the Wolfsschanze and, while discussions continued in Keitel's office, he loitered in the corridor with the explosives. Unsurprisingly for a man involved in a plot to kill the Führer, he appeared a little agitated and was challenged by one of Keitel's NCOs, Oberfeldwebel (Sergeant) Werner Vogel, but Haeften was able to convince him nothing was amiss.

A fuse of the type used by Stauffenberg to detonate the explosives. The complete fuse is shown at the bottom and broken into its component parts above. On the left can be seen the acid in its capsule. When broken the acid would eat through a wire, which would release the spring-loaded firing pin. (NARA)

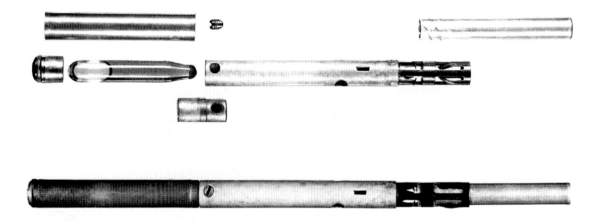

At much the same time, Heinz Linge, Hitler's valet, called Keitel's office to remind him that, because of a visit by Mussolini, the briefing with Hitler had been brought forward by 30 minutes and would now start at 1230hrs. Soon after this message was received, the shuttle railway car from Mauerwald[7] was espied and Major Ernst John von Freyend informed Keitel accordingly. Keitel now brought the meeting to a close, so that he would not be late for Hitler. This posed something of a dilemma for Stauffenberg who needed time to prime the explosives. However, this eventuality had already been anticipated and Stauffenberg asked for time to freshen up and change his shirt. This he did with the help of Haeften, and he then prepared the explosives and fuses.

Stauffenberg and Haeften had two blocks of plastic explosive – more than enough for the task. However, the fuse was difficult to set, especially for a man with only one hand, in spite of the fact that the pliers he used had been specially adapted for his use.[8]

To begin with, the fuse had to be removed from the primer charge. Then the metal casing had to be pinched with pliers to break the glass vial inside, which contained acid that would slowly eat away the wire holding the striker pin. Finally, once this had been done, the safety pin had to be removed and the fuse reinserted in the primer charge.

One pack of explosives had been prepared when they were interrupted by Oberfeldwebel Vogel. Ironically, part of the reason for his interruption was to let them know about a call from General der Nachrichtentruppe (General of Signal Troops) Erich Fellgiebel, a fellow plotter. Vogel remained at the door insisting that Stauffenberg hurry. He received a brusque response, but with no opportunity to prime the second pack of explosives, Stauffenberg dropped the first into his briefcase and composed himself. Haeften concealed the second pack in his briefcase. John von Freyend now called from the entrance for them to hurry up; Keitel and the others were waiting outside and were growing impatient. To help Stauffenberg, John von Freyend offered to carry his briefcase; his offer was firmly but politely declined.

Stauffenberg walked to the briefing with General der Infanterie Walter Buhle, his former commanding officer. When they reached the briefing hut, Stauffenberg passed the briefcase containing the explosives to John von Freyend and asked to be given a place near the Führer, in order to 'catch everything I need for my briefing afterwards' (quoted in Hoffmann 1996: 399). Stauffenberg's hearing had been damaged when he was wounded in North Africa.

When Stauffenberg and the others entered the *Lagezimmer* (briefing room), Generalleutnant Adolf Heusinger was already providing an outline of the situation on the Eastern Front. Keitel announced Stauffenberg and Hitler shook his hand. John von Freyend now placed the briefcase under

---

7   Mauerwald was the location of the OKH; many army attendees would arrive at the Wolfsschanze via this car.
8   It is unclear why Haeften did not help. Stauffenberg may have insisted that he be the sole assassin, or Haeften's beliefs may have been the reason. He had previously rejected killing Hitler because it ran counter to the Fifth Commandment: thou shall not kill (or, in some translations, 'murder').

THE WOLFSSCHANZE: SPERRKREIS I

LOCATIONS 1-30

1. Anti-Aircraft Bunker
2. Boiler House
3. Bormann's Bunker
4. Briefing Hut
5. Bunker
6. Cinema
7. Detective Detail; Post Office
8. Drivers' Quarters
9. Führerbunker
10. Garages
11. General-Purpose Bunker
12. Göring's Bunker
13. Göring's Offices
14. Guest Bunker
15. Hitler's Personal Adjutants' Offices;
    Army Personnel Office
16. Jodl's Offices
17. Keitel's Bunker
18. Liaison, Medical and Support Offices
19. New Teahouse
20. Officers' Mess I
21. Officers' Mess II
22. Old Teahouse
23. Press Bunker
24. RSD and SS barracks
25. Sauna
26. Security Building
27. Signals Bunker
28. SS-Begleit-Kommando; Servants' Quarters
29. Stenographers' Offices
30. Water Reservoir (for fighting fires)

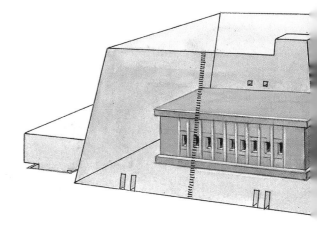

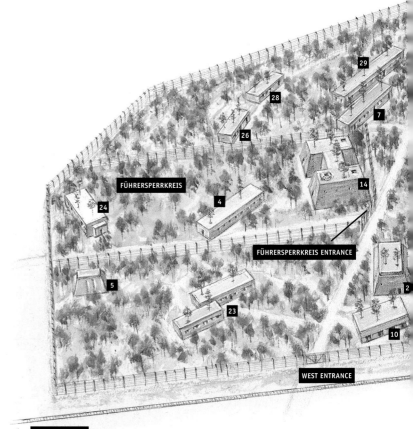

FÜHRERSPERRKREIS

FÜHRERSPERRKREIS ENTRANCE

WEST ENTRANCE

TO RASTENBURG

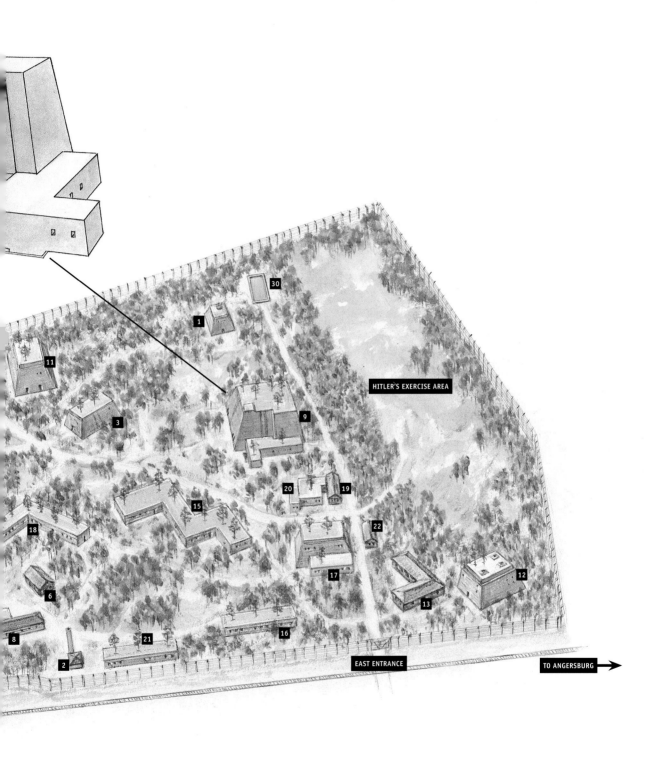

30

1

11

3

9

HITLER'S EXERCISE AREA

20   19

15

22

18

17

6

12

8   13

2   21   16

EAST ENTRANCE   TO ANGERSBURG →

The briefing on 20 July was held in the briefing hut. This was a long, low building with the briefing room at one end. This was reached by means of a long corridor that ran down the centre of the building (shown). The blast was such that the doors along the length of the corridor were damaged. (Topfoto)

the table and Stauffenberg took his place next to Heusinger, who was in turn next to Hitler. Konteradmiral Hans-Erich Voss, representing the Kriegsmarine commander-in-chief, Grossadmiral Karl Dönitz, moved to the other side of the table. The briefing resumed and Hitler leant over the table, magnifying glass in hand. Stauffenberg now surreptitiously moved the briefcase as close to Hitler as possible, but recognized that one of the substantial legs of the table was in the way. To have tried to place it any closer would have aroused suspicion.

View from the entrance to the briefing room towards the windows at the end of the block. It was the height of summer and in the middle of the day so all the windows were open, which helped to dissipate the blast. Even then, the damage was extensive. (NARA)

The first part of the mission complete, Stauffenberg signalled to John von Freyend that he needed to make a call and the two of them exited the room. John von Freyend asked the telephone operator, Wachtmeister (Sergeant-Major) Arthur Adam, to call Fellgiebel and then returned to the briefing. Stauffenberg didn't wait for the connection, but left the building (leaving his hat and belt) and went off to the *Adjutantenhaus* (adjutant's building), which was some 200m from the briefing hut. Here he met Fellgiebel and Haeften, who in the interim had been finalizing arrangements

The explosives were left in a briefcase, which was placed on the floor near Hitler. When the explosives were detonated the force of blast moved out from the epicentre, but did little damage to the floor. The carpet was damaged and a small hole blown in the floorboards. (NARA)

20 JULY 1944
1015hrs

Stauffenberg arrives at the Wolfsschanze

20 JULY 1944
1230hrs

Conference with Hitler begins

20 JULY 1944
1242hrs

Bomb explodes

for the car to take them to the airfield. This had been supplied with the intention of taking Stauffenberg for a lunch appointment with Oberstleutnant Gustav Streve, the camp commandant. However, Streve was about to be disappointed; his lunch date had another more pressing engagement in Berlin.

As Stauffenberg and Fellgiebel left the office the explosives detonated, startling both of them; Oberstleutnant Sander, the Wehrmacht signals officer, was unsurprised, however, believing it to be one of the mines laid around the perimeter being detonated by an unlucky animal. Stauffenberg, knowing the truth, explained he would not return to the conference but would go straight to lunch. He bade farewell and stepped into his car along with Haeften. The driver, Leutnant Erich Kretz, noticed that Stauffenberg had forgotten his hat and belt, but Stauffenberg insisted he drive on. As they headed off, Stauffenberg and Haeften could see smoke emanating from the briefing hut and figures running to and from the scene. Amid the chaos, they saw someone carried out under Hitler's cloak. Stauffenberg was sure that this was the Führer. He was mistaken, however; fearing a further explosion, Hitler had been spirited away to his bunker.

Only a few minutes earlier the briefing room had been a picture of calm. After Stauffenberg left the conference, Oberst Heinz Brandt, who was standing next to him, pushed the briefcase a little further under the table so that it was not in his way, but he did not move it to the other side of the leg as is sometimes suggested. Heusinger continued to provide his update on the Eastern Front and, during his presentation, a point was raised that Stauffenberg would have been able to answer, but he was absent. Buhle went looking for him, but could only ascertain from Wachtmeister Adam that Stauffenberg had left the building. Then, just after 1240hrs, the bomb exploded. Warlimont recalled:

In a flash the map room became a scene of stampede and destruction. At one moment was to be seen a set of men and things which together formed a focal point of world events; at the next there was nothing but wounded men groaning, the acrid smell of burning, and charred fragments of maps and papers fluttering in the wind. (Warlimont n.d.: 440)

The explosion had blown a hole in the floor and had wrecked the heavy table. The plasterboard covering the walls and ceiling had been badly damaged and the glass fibre behind was strewn around the room.

The reckoning

Everyone in the room tried to escape the carnage; there was the very real danger that there might have been another bomb or that the roof might collapse. Warlimont scrambled through a window. Once outside he regained his composure and was aware that Oberst Brandt was also trying to escape from the devastated room. However, he had been so badly injured that he was unable to extricate himself and had to be helped to safety by John von Freyend – a feat von Freyend repeated in also rescuing the badly injured Generalleutnant Schmundt. Once outside and away from the danger, John von Freyend proceeded to cut away Schmundt's boot so that his wounds could be treated. Meanwhile, Warlimont attempted to re-enter the building to collect his papers, but by this time the area had been secured by SS guards and when he did make it into the briefing room he collapsed and had to be evacuated by his personal staff.

View of the briefing room taken from in front of the windows at the far end of the block. The force of the blast was such that it demolished one of the internal stud walls, behind which was the telephone room. The smaller round table in the conference room is just visible on the left. (NARA)

Like Warlimont, Oberst Nicolaus von Below had also made a miraculous escape. At the start of the meeting he was away from the main table, discussing the visit of Mussolini with the other adjutants. However, Heusinger made an interesting point and Below moved to study the map. At that point the bomb exploded and he was momentarily knocked unconscious. When he came round he was greeted by a scene of utter devastation. Recognizing the danger, he exited through a window and made his way to the front entrance, where he witnessed some of the injured being removed from the building. Eleven attendees were hospitalized, the remainder suffering minor injuries including burst eardrums.

Astonishingly, Keitel, who was on Hitler's left at the briefing, was unhurt and, though shocked, soon regained his senses and immediately called after Hitler. Searching through the dust and smoke he found him and led him out. Aside from his clothing, which had been shredded, he seemed fine. Hitler's personal aide, SS-Gruppenführer Julius Schaub, and the Führer's valet, SS-Obersturmführer Heinz Linge, hurried to the scene and helped Hitler back to his bunker for a medical examination. This was initially conducted by Professor von Hasselbach who dressed the Führer's wounds, but he was later relieved by Doctor Morell, Hitler's personal physician, and Hasselbach headed for Karlshof hospital near Rastenburg to treat the others wounded in the blast.

Isolating the Wolfsschanze

While the wounded were being evacuated to hospital, Below made his way to the *Nachrichtenbunker* (signals bunker), where he explained what had happened to the duty officer, Oberleutnant Hans Hornbogen. He in turn called Oberstleutnant Ludolf Sander, the Wehrmacht signals officer, who immediately returned to the exchange. When he arrived he ordered that no

Hitler after the assassination attempt, apparently showing no signs of physical injury. Just behind him is Bormann, his private secretary, who was not at the conference. To Hitler's left is Generaloberst Jodl with his head bandaged, and behind him is Oberst von Below, one of Hitler's adjutants, who was also slightly injured. (Topfoto)

messages were to be sent unless from Hitler, Keitel or Generaloberst Alfred Jodl, OKW Chief of Operations. This was a stroke of luck for Fellgiebel, whose orders from the conspirators in the Bendlerblock were to stop all communication from the Wolfsschanze so that the conspirators could enact *Valkyrie*. Although Fellgiebel was head of army and Wehrmacht communications, his authority over the latter was limited and it would have been difficult for him, without support at a more junior level, to establish a communications blackout.

The Führer takes stock

From the signals bunker, Below, still slightly concussed, walked the short distance to Hitler's quarters in the guest bunker. Hitler was still in shock, but was sufficiently compos mentis to ask his adjutant how he was and to affirm that they had all been very lucky (at this point he was unaware of the fatalities). At about the same time Hitler received a number of other visitors, including his secretaries, Traudl Junge and Christa Schroeder.

At lunchtime all the secretaries had been in their rooms. The Wolfsschanze was quiet but the peace was broken by an explosion. This was alarming but not unusual, because there was building work going on and weapons were often tested. And, like Oberstleutnant Sander, they were aware that occasionally wild animals would set off one of the land mines protecting the site, so they took little notice and carried on with their duties. However, it soon became clear that something was wrong as Traudl Junge heard calls for a doctor. She left her room and spoke to two orderlies coming from Hitler's compound, who explained that there had been an explosion.

Junge now ran towards the briefing room and met Jodl, who was covered in blood. Concussed and with burst eardrums, Jodl could not understand Junge, and security staff now ushered onlookers away. Fearing the worst, Junge went back to her room. Minutes later SS-Sturmbannführer Otto Günsche, Hitler's personal adjutant, passed the secretaries' quarters. He seemed fine and Junge spoke to him. He confirmed there had been an explosion, and hypothesized that a rogue Organization Todt worker, employed to reinforce the buildings, had planted a bomb. Reassuringly, he confirmed that the Führer was fine and suggested that Junge go to Hitler's bunker, which she did.

When she arrived, she found the Führer looking a little dishevelled, but alive: 'His hair … was standing on end so that he looked like a hedgehog. His black trousers were hanging in strips from his belt, almost like a raffia skirt'. His right arm was badly bruised, so he greeted her with his left and explained that this was 'Yet more proof that Fate has chosen me for my mission …' (Junge 2004: 130).

Christa Schroeder also visited Hitler that afternoon. He welcomed her with a little difficulty, but aside from that he seemed fine. He explained that 'The heavy table leg diverted the explosion … I had extraordinary luck! If the explosion had happened in the bunker and not in the wooden hut, nobody would have survived …' (Schroeder 2009: 122). Hitler then showed his secretary his shredded trousers and asked that they be sent to the Berghof where they should be carefully preserved.

Overleaf:
On 20 July 1944 Oberst Claus Schenk Graf von Stauffenberg travelled to the Wolfsschanze ostensibly to brief Hitler on the state of the Replacement Army. However, among his papers Stauffenberg also had explosives and detonators which he was to use to kill Hitler. The plan was simple. At the briefing he would place the bomb, now primed and secreted in his briefcase, next to Hitler before making his excuses to leave. The bomb would explode killing Hitler and his immediate circle of advisors. With the Führer dead the conspirators would introduce martial law, seizing key buildings and arresting those loyal to Hitler. Once power had been wrested from the Nazis a new government would be introduced which would seek to end the war. The bomb exploded as planned, but unbeknown to Stauffenberg, who had left the room and was now heading to Berlin, Hitler survived with only minor injuries. As the dust settled, it soon became clear what had happened and with communication links still open Hitler was able to confirm that he was safe and well and his supporters quickly rounded up the conspirators, who were tried and executed.

An orderly holds the trousers that Hitler was wearing at the briefing on 20 July. The devastating power of the blast is clear from the way the trousers have been shredded. Surprisingly, Hitler received relatively few injuries. (Topfoto)

Hitler's injured right arm was in fact a bruised elbow; he had also suffered minor burns to his legs and his left hand had abrasions. Both of his eardrums had burst and, although his ears were bloody, his hearing did not appear to be affected. Patched up, Hitler retired to his room and changed, ready to greet the Duce who was due in an hour. Soon afterwards, Fellgiebel saw Hitler walking inside his compound. Shocked, he called Generalleutnant Fritz Thiele, his chief of staff at OKW in Berlin, with his news. Thiele now spoke to Olbricht, who in turn contacted General der Artillerie Eduard Wagner, Deputy Chief of the Army General Staff at Zossen (the site of the OKH headquarters, located 30km south of Berlin). They agreed that they would do nothing until they had definitive news either way concerning Hitler's fate.

Stauffenberg and Haeften return to Berlin

While this was going on, Stauffenberg and Haeften made their way to the airfield, convinced that their mission had been a success. They negotiated the first checkpoint relatively easily; the guards had lowered the barrier on hearing the explosion, but with no reason to stop anyone they allowed Stauffenberg to pass. The two conspirators and their driver now made their way to the outer perimeter and the final checkpoint before the airfield. This proved more problematic. By the time they reached this gate the alarm had been sounded and the headquarters was in lockdown. Nothing was allowed in or out. Stauffenberg's powers of persuasion did not sway the guards. A call was made to Rittmeister von Möllendorff, who had had breakfast with Stauffenberg that morning. Assuming that his dining companion had urgent business in Berlin, he ordered that he be allowed to pass, although he did not have authority to do this. The barrier was raised and the driver accelerated away. They now made haste to Rastenburg Airfield and on the way took the opportunity to dispose of the unused explosives. The driver saw a package being thrown into the undergrowth, but thought little of it at the time and dropped his passengers safely at their destination. Wagner's He 111 was waiting for them, fuelled and ready to go, and at 1315hrs they took off.

With the situation in the signals bunker secure, Oberstleutnant Sander made his way to the briefing hut to check on the equipment there. Wachtmeister Adam was still at his post, although clearly there was nothing to do as far as his communications role was concerned. He asked permission to speak to Sander and explained that Stauffenberg had left the conference immediately before the explosion, implying that the officer was in some way involved. Sander was outraged and explained he wanted to hear nothing more of the tale, and that if he was convinced of his facts he should speak to security. Adam did better than that: he spoke to Martin Bormann, Hitler's private secretary, who ushered him in to speak to Hitler. Adam's story proved to be correct and he was handsomely rewarded with a promotion, money and a house.

A search for Stauffenberg was ordered. However, it soon became clear that he had boarded a plane at Rastenburg and had left the headquarters. The driver who had taken Stauffenberg to the airfield was now questioned. He confirmed that Stauffenberg had flown out and that something had been thrown from the car on the journey. Troops were immediately ordered to check the roadside, where they found the discarded explosives. Stauffenberg was clearly implicated in the plot and Himmler was now made responsible for bringing him, and any other conspirators, to justice. Himmler had been ordered to the Führer's presence, along with Göring, immediately after the explosion, but they were not told what had happened. Once briefed, Himmler and SS-Obergruppenführer Dr Ernst Kaltenbrunner, head of the Reichsicherheitshauptamt (RSHA – Reich Central Security Office), set off for Berlin, flown by SS-Obersturmbannführer Adolf Doldi, one of SS-Brigadeführer Hans Baur's pilots (Baur was chief pilot to Hitler), who had come straight from the dentist.

The briefing hut was a simple prefabricated structure. The walls were made from wooden slats with plasterboard on the inside. Between the two was a layer of fibreglass for insulation, remnants of which can just be seen. A bullet-proof coating was added to the outside. (NARA)

Mussolini was due for a meeting with Hitler on 20 July. Following the bomb blast Hitler invited the Duce to inspect the damage with him. The two leaders are standing at the end of the corridor leading to the briefing room. On the right is the chief interpreter at the Foreign Office, Dr Paul Otto Schmidt. (Topfoto)

Opposite Berlin and its environs, 20 July 1944. Deutschlandersender III at Herzberg lies to the south – see the map on page 47.

20 JULY 1944 1315hrs

Stauffenberg and Haeften fly out of Rastenburg

20 JULY 1944 1330hrs

Fellgiebel calls the Bendlerblock: 'The Führer is alive'

20 JULY 1944 1400hrs

Mertz von Quirnheim initiates first part of *Valkyrie*

Patched up and changed, Hitler prepared to greet Mussolini. The two met at Görlitz station at 1430hrs. Hitler greeted his visitor, exclaiming, 'Duce! I have just had the most enormous stroke of good fortune' (quoted in Irving 2002: 703). He explained what had happened and took Mussolini to the scene of his miraculous escape, before returning to business, briefing the Duce about the war effort, including the new V-2 rockets that would soon enter service. At 1700hrs Hitler sat down for tea with Mussolini.

Soon after, a call came through from Goebbels in Berlin. It was clear that moves were afoot to unseat Hitler and he asked the propaganda minister to broadcast a message confirming he was alive. The conversation at the tea party resumed and was dominated by the attempt on Hitler's life. The exchanges became increasingly heated as Grossadmiral Dönitz and Joachim von Ribbentrop, the foreign minister, criticized the generals for their betrayal. Hitler sat quietly for the most part, but at one point mention was made of the Röhm plot of 30 June 1934. At this, Hitler sprang to life and threatened vengeance on the traitors. His diatribe lasted a full 30 minutes, before he settled back in his seat. The silence was filled by his cohorts, who pledged allegiance to Hitler in increasingly overblown terms that culminated in a fierce argument between Göring and Ribbentrop. At 1900hrs the tea party concluded and Mussolini left – the two leaders would never meet again.

The conspirators' dilemma

Back in Berlin, the plotters awaited word from the Wolfsschanze, but when it came it was ambiguous. Fellgiebel reported that 'Something terrible has happened, the Führer is alive' (quoted in Hoffmann 2008: 268). To Thiele and Olbricht this could mean one of two things. It could be that the bomb had not been detonated (as had been the case before), or that Stauffenberg had been discovered. If the latter was true then it was likely that Stauffenberg had either been killed by Hitler's bodyguards, or he had done the honourable thing and committed suicide to protect his co-conspirators. What they do not appear to have considered is the possibility that the bomb had detonated, but that Hitler had survived.

Having dismissed this alternative, or never considered it feasible in the first instance, they believed that the best course of action was inactivity. After the events of 15 July, they certainly could not order an alert. Fromm had been furious the last time and certainly would not endorse an order to mobilize when the message from the Wolfsschanze was equivocal. Neither could Olbricht and Thiele act independently; the Führer was, after all, seemingly alive and as such there were no special circumstances that might incline those asked to act to actually do so. No, they would carry on as normal, and so they went to lunch. Once definitive news had been received, then they would act – not beforehand. Not until 1500hrs did they return to the office. In stark contrast, Oberst Mertz von Quirnheim, who had heard the news of Hitler's survival at the same time, was far more proactive and pressed ahead with the first part of *Valkyrie*. At about 1400hrs he sent out the orders to place units on alert.

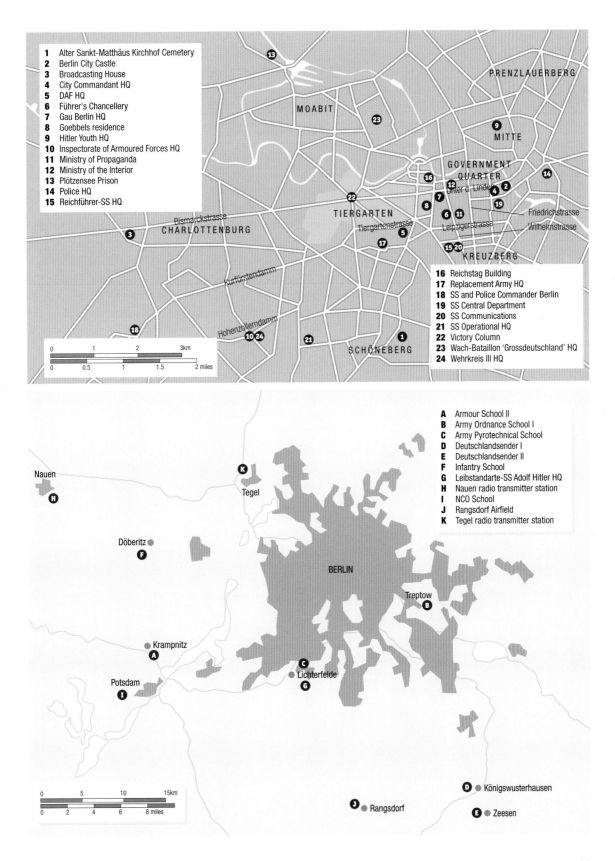

1 Alter Sankt-Matthäus Kirchhof Cemetery
2 Berlin City Castle
3 Broadcasting House
4 City Commandant HQ
5 DAF HQ
6 Führer's Chancellery
7 Gau Berlin HQ
8 Goebbels residence
9 Hitler Youth HQ
10 Inspectorate of Armoured Forces HQ
11 Ministry of Propaganda
12 Ministry of the Interior
13 Plötzensee Prison
14 Police HQ
15 Reichführer-SS HQ

16 Reichstag Building
17 Replacement Army HQ
18 SS and Police Commander Berlin
19 SS Central Department
20 SS Communications
21 SS Operational HQ
22 Victory Column
23 Wach-Bataillon 'Grossdeutschland' HQ
24 Wehrkreis III HQ

A Armour School II
B Army Ordnance School I
C Army Pyrotechnical School
D Deutschlandsender I
E Deutschlandsender II
F Infantry School
G Leibstandarte-SS Adolf Hitler HQ
H Nauen radio transmitter station
I NCO School
J Rangsdorf Airfield
K Tegel radio transmitter station

PRENZLAUERBERG
MOABIT
MITTE
GOVERNMENT QUARTER
Unter d. Linden
Friedrichstrasse
Wilhelmstrasse
TIERGARTEN
Tiergartenstrasse
Leipzigerstrasse
Bismarckstrasse
CHARLOTTENBURG
KREUZBERG
Kurfürstendamm
Hohenzollerndamm
SCHÖNEBERG

Nauen
Tegel
Döberitz
Krampnitz
Potsdam
BERLIN
Treptow
Lichterfelde
Königswusterhausen
Rangsdorf
Zeesen

Arrival in Berlin

At about 1545hrs, Stauffenberg and Haeften arrived at Berlin's Rangsdorf Airfield, but when they alighted they found their transport was not there. Schweizer had gone to the airport, but for reasons that are unclear he missed his passengers. Stauffenberg spoke to the officer in charge at the airfield (having done a trial run, he knew him) and managed to get a car. During the delay, Haeften called ahead to the Bendlerblock to confirm Hitler's death. With no sense that a different version of events had percolated through from the Wolfsschanze, they now set off to drive the 30km to the Bendlerblock, arriving at 1630hrs.

Once Mertz von Quirnheim was aware of Stauffenberg's arrival in Berlin, he pressed Olbricht to set in motion the second stage of *Valkyrie*. Olbricht still prevaricated, but eventually decided to accept that the Führer had been killed. Mertz von Quirnheim now briefed the staff in the Bendlerblock that Hitler was dead, that Beck was Staatsoberhaupt (Head of State) and that Generalfeldmarschall Erwin von Witzleben was now Wehrmacht Commander-in-Chief. At just before 1600hrs the codeword 'Valkyrie Stage 2' was issued to all *Wehrkreise* (military districts) and, importantly, to the various units in Berlin. At the same time the orders were removed from the safe for Fromm to sign, and both Mertz von Quirnheim and Olbricht went to see the commander of the Replacement Army.

The two officers explained the situation to Fromm, but understandably after the debacle only five days before he was reluctant to sign. Anticipating this, and now convinced that Stauffenberg's view of events was correct, Olbricht organized an urgent call to Keitel. Fromm spoke to Keitel, explaining that rumours were circulating in Berlin concerning the Führer's wellbeing. Keitel confirmed that there had been an explosion, but that Hitler was fine. Keitel now turned from the quizzed to the quizzer, asking after Stauffenberg's whereabouts. Fromm replied that he had not yet returned to Berlin.

During the attempted coup on 20 July, Goebbels was in Berlin where he was instrumental in crushing the uprising. However, once the danger had passed, he visited Hitler at the Wolfsschanze. Göring and Goebbels are shown the damage by Hitler. SS-Gruppenführer Hermann Fegelein, who was at the conference, is in the foreground. (Topfoto)

Unperturbed, Olbricht and Mertz von Quirnheim left Fromm and, at 1630hrs, they issued a general order to all *Wehrkreise*. It was from Witzleben and stated:

> The Führer Adolf Hitler is dead ... In order to maintain law and order in this situation of acute danger the Reich Government has declared a state of martial law and has transferred the executive power to me together with the supreme command of the Wehrmacht ... Any resistance against the military authorities is to be ruthlessly suppressed. (Quoted in Noakes 2010: 621)

The length of the message (the passage above is abridged), the number of addressees and the fact that the text had to be entered into the Enigma encoding machines meant it took an incredible amount of time and effort to send. Consequently, it didn't arrive in some military districts until much later in the day, when some key officers had gone home. They had to be contacted and then make their way to their respective headquarters, adding further to the delay in implementing the order. Witzleben's order was followed by a further message calling on units to secure key buildings (radio stations, telephone exchanges, etc.) and for the arrest of party officials (at *Gauleiter*,[9] minister and governor levels) and senior Gestapo and SS officers.

Stauffenberg confronts Fromm

When Stauffenberg arrived at the Bendlerblock he reiterated that Hitler was dead and at the same time was brought up to speed on developments in Berlin, not least Fromm's intransigence. Stauffenberg and Olbricht went to see Fromm and once again Stauffenberg confirmed what he had seen and stated categorically that Hitler was dead. Fromm challenged his version of events based on his discussion with Keitel, to which Stauffenberg countered that Keitel was one of Hitler's lackeys and was always lying. Olbricht now confirmed that the *Valkyrie* order had been issued. Fromm was outraged; he slammed the desk and in no uncertain terms made it clear that what they were doing amounted to treason, the penalty for which was death.

Fromm now demanded to know who had issued the *Valkyrie* order. Olbricht explained it was Mertz von Quirnheim, and he was now summoned to Fromm's presence where he confirmed that he had indeed issued the order. Understanding the full implications of what had happened, Fromm sought to save himself and ordered the plotters be placed under arrest. Stauffenberg, the picture of calm, ignored this idle threat and reiterated that the Führer was dead. Fromm vigorously disagreed and suggested the honourable thing for Stauffenberg to do was shoot himself; Stauffenberg declined. A scuffle ensued, and Fromm, having been given one last chance to join the coup, was relieved of his duties and was placed under house arrest.

---

9   A *Gauleiter* was the head of a *Gau*, an archaic German term revived by the Nazis and used to designate a political region.

The Wehrkreise: Events on 20 July 1944

I (Königsberg): Units engaged in anti-partisan duties so few troops available and as such could not carry out orders even if they wanted to. Commander, General der Artillerie Albert Wodrig, spoke to neighbouring *Wehrkreise*, who were doing nothing. Spoke to Keitel who insisted that the only orders to be followed were from the Wolfsschanze. Stauffenberg's call not taken.

II (Stettin): Commander, General der Infanterie Werner Kienitz, sympathetic to coup. Received teleprint and called neighbouring *Wehrkreise*. Situation unclear so waited. Received call from Keitel explaining what had happened. Later called by Hoepner and Olbricht and told to follow *Valkyrie* orders. Keitel outranked them so this direction was ignored.

III (Berlin): See main narrative.

IV (Dresden): Received teleprint orders. Headquarters secured and troops put on alert. At same time received a call from Keitel who explained all messages from Berlin were to be ignored. Phoned neighbouring *Wehrkreise*, who had adopted a 'wait and see' approach. Then heard radio message about coup and Hitler's survival – nothing more done.

V (Stuttgart): Teleprints arrived late, decoding took time and the revolt had already collapsed before decisions could be taken. No units alerted.

VI (Münster): First teleprint order arrived. Before second message the operations officer, Oberst Kuhn, spoke to Stauffenberg, who explained formal orders would follow and should be adhered to. Keitel called and explained Hitler was well and orders from Berlin were to be ignored. No units mobilized.

VII (Munich): No orders received from Berlin before coup had effectively ended due to the heavy Allied bombing. When Keitel called in the evening he was told all was quiet.

VIII (Breslau): Units occupied with anti-partisan duties so few available for *Valkyrie*. When Stauffenberg called, chief of staff, Generalmajor Ludwig Freiherr Rüdt von Collenberg, had not seen the orders. Stauffenberg did not elaborate. Generalleutnant Wilhelm Burgdorf, deputy head of the Heerespersonalamt (Army Personnel Office), called and told Collenberg to ignore orders from Berlin. Called other *Wehrkreise*. The message was the same; Hitler was alive, do nothing.

IX (Kassel): Plans in this *Wehrkreis* were more advanced because a number of the officers in charge were part of the conspiracy. When the order came, the commander, General der Infanterie Otto Schellert, was away and did not return until late. Briefed by his chief of staff, Oberst Claus-Henning von Plate, and, in spite of the contradictory messages received, Schellert

did issue the *Valkyrie* order and some buildings were secured. However, after a call from Keitel and having spoken to other *Wehrkreise*, it became clear to Schellert that the coup had failed and the orders were cancelled.

X (Hamburg): Both the commander, General der Infanterie Wilhelm Wetzel, and chief of staff, Generalmajor Friedrich-Wilhelm Prüter, were absent when the teleprint arrived ordering the commencement of *Valkyrie*. When Prüter returned to the headquarters he put units on alert. Later he rang other neighbouring *Wehrkreise* and found they had not acted. The few orders that had been issued were later cancelled as it became clear that Hitler was alive and the coup had failed.

XI (Hanover): Teleprints arrived late, decoding took time and the revolt had already collapsed before decisions could be taken. The commander, General der Infanterie Benno Bieler, called Stauffenberg but did not get a satisfactory answer to all his questions. Later Keitel called Bieler to explain Hitler was alive and that the coup was being crushed. He decided not to act.

XII (Wiesbaden): Teleprints arrived late, decoding took time and the revolt had already collapsed before decisions could be taken.

XIII (Nuremberg): Teleprints arrived late. Commander, General der Infanterie Mauritz von Wiktorin, spoke to Berlin and the Wolfsschanze and received contradictory orders, so adopted a 'wait and see' approach.

XVII (Vienna): See main narrative.

XVIII (Salzburg): Teleprints arrived late. Oberst Glasl, chief of staff, heard from the Wolfsschanze that Hitler was alive before hearing that Hitler had been assassinated. No action was taken.

XX (Danzig): Commander was Keitel's brother, General der Infanterie Bodewin Keitel. *Wehrkreis* close to front and Keitel on inspection when orders arrived. Later checked with sibling and situation explained. Did nothing to enact orders from Berlin.

XXI (Posen): *Wehrkreis* close to combat zone and no reserve units to speak of. Most senior officers on tours of inspection, so teleprints not seen till late. Clear that no action being taken in other *Wehrkreise* and Burgdorf called to confirm Hitler was alive. No action taken.

Böhmen und Mähren (Prague): See main narrative.

General Government (Krakow): Orders were received by Generalmajor Max Bork, the chief of staff, but by the time they arrived he had already heard the radio messages of the Führer's survival. At 2200hrs Stieff called to say orders from Berlin were to be ignored. When Burgdorf called, Bork explained that orders had been received but had not been actioned, thanks to Stieff.

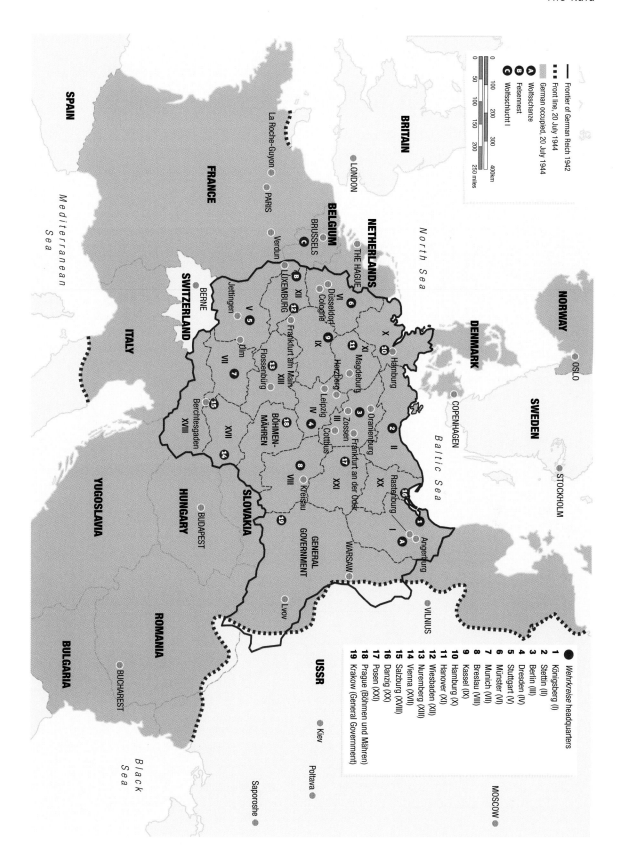

After this explosive episode, the situation in the Bendlerblock settled down. The orders had been issued and the plotters now had to wait for the troops to mobilize. Following Fromm's arrest, another message was sent detailing the appointment of Hoepner as commander of the Replacement Army; later still, advice was issued insisting that the radio broadcasts talking of Hitler's survival were wrong and that the *Valkyrie* orders should be carried out with the utmost speed. Meanwhile, Beck and Hoepner had now appeared at the Bendlerblock. Both arrived in civilian clothes, Beck to avoid suspicion of a coup and Hoepner because in December 1941 Hitler had denied him the privilege of wearing uniform. Both now took up their respective positions in the new regime: Beck as Head of State and Hoepner as commander of the Replacement Army. Hoepner made his way to Fromm's office and spoke to the man he had replaced. Fromm's view had not changed. Hitler was still alive, he insisted, and it was a mistake to continue with the *Putsch* (*coup d'état*). It was too late, however – the orders had been issued.

Meanwhile, Beck spoke to General der Artillerie Wagner at Zossen, explaining the situation and stating that Witzleben would soon be with him to take over as commander-in-chief of the Wehrmacht. The Bendlerblock was the headquarters for the Replacement Army, where most of the plotters worked, but Zossen, the OKH headquarters, was much better equipped for the commander-in-chief to direct operations. After this call Wagner received a call from Stieff at the Wolfsschanze. Stieff understood that the *Valkyrie* orders had been issued, but he was also aware that Hitler had survived and insisted that to continue was madness. Wagner now asked Stieff to tell Keitel what was happening and of the calls Wagner had received from the Bendlerblock. Later, Wagner stated that he had never supported the coup, but this attempt to cover his trail – he had lent Stauffenberg his aircraft after all – did not save him. He committed suicide on 23 July.

Success and failure in the *Wehrkreise*

While this was going on, Stauffenberg focussed his energies on maintaining the momentum in the coup. He called the various military districts and reiterated that Hitler was dead and what the orders were. However, the reaction to the *Valkyrie* orders was patchy (see previous pages).

Events in Vienna

The first teleprint from Berlin arrived in Vienna at about 1800hrs, when most of the senior officers had left. On reading the message Oberst Heinrich Kodré, chief of staff, contacted the acting commander, General der Panzertruppe (General of Armoured Troops) Hans-Karl Freiherr von Esebeck, and requested he return to Wehrkreis XVII headquarters, which he did. At the same time a platoon of Wach-Bataillon Wien (Vienna Guard Battalion) was ordered to deploy around the headquarters. This was followed by the receipt of the second teleprint from Berlin ordering the arrest of Nazi officials, SS and SD personnel. As a first step Kodré ordered all senior officers in Wehrkreis XVII to report to the Old War Ministry (the Kriegministerium, located in Vienna's Stubenring) for a conference at 1900hrs.

When Esebeck arrived, he read the messages and agreed with Kodré that they should be followed, but just to double-check Kodré rang Stauffenberg, his counterpart in Berlin, who confirmed that the orders were correct and urged him to enact them with the utmost speed. By now the senior officers (or their deputies) had begun to arrive at the Old War Ministry. At 1920hrs the conference began. Those present were briefed on developments and were directed to enact the *Valkyrie* order in their respective areas. Generalleutnant Adolf Sinzinger, City Commandant of Vienna, was tasked with arresting party dignitaries and senior SS officers. However, rather than frogmarch the accused to Wehrkreis XVII headquarters, they were to be invited and then detained; force was only to be used as a last resort.

Understandably, some of the individuals invited to the Old War Ministry were suspicious about the request, especially at this late hour. Most did turn up, though some had to be cajoled into entering the building and others came armed. When they were all assembled they were briefed on the orders received and specifically the order to arrest them. They accepted that Esebeck was only doing his duty and submitted to incarceration, the inconvenience being eased by the provision of brandy and cigars.

As part of the investigation into the bomb plot, evidence was gathered to establish how the attack was carried out and by whom. These are the pliers that were used by Stauffenberg to break the glass vial that would detonate the explosives. They were left in the briefcase and damaged in the blast. (NARA)

A teleprint was now received in Wehrkreis XVII headquarters detailing the appointment of political representatives to take up key roles in the city. These individuals were known to be unsympathetic to the regime, which raised doubts in Esebeck's mind about what was going on. These concerns were heightened with the receipt of a further message stating that the radio message talking of Hitler's survival was untrue. If any doubt remained, it was swept away by a telephone call from Keitel, who impressed on Kodré and Esebeck in no uncertain terms that Hitler was alive and that the orders from Berlin were not to be followed. In a later call, Stauffenberg tried to convince Kodré of the need to keep his nerve, but the call was cut off. Kodré and Esebeck tried to call Witzleben, but without success; later they spoke to Burgdorf, who confirmed that a *Putsch* had been attempted but it had been unsuccessful and power still rested with Hitler. The *Valkyrie* orders were now cancelled and all the prisoners were released. The following day Esebeck, Sinzinger and Kodré explained themselves to Baldur von Schirach, the *Gauleiter*, but without success and they were imprisoned until the end of the war.

Events in Prague

Oddly, the adherence to the *Valkyrie* order was much more successful outside Germany and Austria. This was surprising because the German units in Czechoslovakia and France were in 'occupied' countries and were therefore surrounded by a population that was hostile to German forces of whatever hue. There was consequently a very real danger that any *Putsch* could lead to internal unrest.

20 JULY 1944
1630hrs

Stauffenberg and
Haeften arrive at
Bendlerblock

20 JULY 1944
1645hrs

Stauffenberg and
Olbricht meet
Fromm; Fromm
arrested

In Prague, General der Panzertruppe Ferdinand Schaal, the commander of *Wehrkreis Böhmen und Mähren* (Bohemia and Moravia), heard of the assassination attempt while at a reception. The message had come from a radio broadcast that suggested Hitler had survived the attempt. Schaal returned to his headquarters where he received the *Valkyrie* order. Confused, he tried to speak to Fromm but was put through to Stauffenberg, who confirmed that Hitler was dead and told him to implement the emergency powers immediately. Schaal mobilized his troops and secured strategic locations, but, before he took further steps to arrest senior Nazis, SD and SS figures, he tried to call Karl Hermann Frank, the German Minister of State for Bohemia and Moravia. Schaal's logic was simple: the SS was stronger than the army in Prague and any arrests would undermine security in the city.

By the time the two men eventually spoke, Frank had received word from the Wolfsschanze that he was only to act on orders from the Führer. Schaal and Frank agreed to meet at a neutral location to discuss the matter, but before Schaal left he, too, received a call from the Wolfsschanze informing him of the coup and that only orders from Keitel and Himmler, the new head of the Replacement Army, were to be obeyed. With this new information he met with Frank and it was agreed that no further action would be taken. When Schaal visited Frank the next day he was also arrested and detained until the end of the war.

Indecision in France

In Paris the orders were successfully implemented, due in no small part to the fact that a number of senior officers were actively involved in, or at least aware of, the plot.

On the afternoon of 20 July General der Infanterie Günther Blumentritt, chief of staff to Commander-in-Chief West, was informed that Hitler was dead and that a new interim government had been formed. Blumentritt tried to contact Generalfeldmarschall Kluge, who had been appointed commander-in-chief west on 2 July 1944, at La Roche-Guyon. However, Kluge was at the front and the call was taken by Generalleutnant Dr Hans Speidel, Army Group B's chief of staff. However, because Blumentritt was not aware of the plot, he did not explain to Speidel what the call concerned and instead drove to La Roche-Guyon to await the return of Kluge.

Meanwhile in Paris, Oberstleutnant Cäsar von Hofacker, who was one of the conspirators, received news from Stauffenberg that the coup was under way; Hofacker immediately briefed his commander, General der Infanterie Carl-Heinrich von Stülpnagel, commander-in-chief France. Stülpnagel acted directly, calling in his senior officers, including Generalleutnant Hans Freiherr von Boineburg-Lengsfeld, the City Commandant of Paris, who was ordered to arrest all SS personnel. This he did, but to ensure these troops would be in their barracks – and to avoid the local populace witnessing an unseemly struggle between Germans – he ordered that it take place after dark. When Kluge returned to his headquarters he spoke to Beck, who briefed him about the events of the day and stressed the importance of Kluge's involvement. In response Kluge asked for time to think and after the call he asked Stülpnagel to come to La Roche-Guyon for a conference.

While Kluge pondered his next move, reports arrived of a radio broadcast stating that Hitler was alive. Kluge now called Generalmajor Stieff, an old colleague, at Mauerwald, and asked him what he knew. Stieff confirmed that Hitler was alive. Still not convinced, Kluge called Fromm in Berlin, but was passed to Generaloberst Hoepner, who maintained the radio reports were wrong and that Hitler was dead. Kluge was understandably confused; he now received orders from Berlin calling on the army to take control and arrest SS units and, importantly, stating that the radio messages reporting that Hitler was alive were untrue.

By this time Blumentritt had arrived and, buoyed by the news, Kluge discussed with him plans for agreeing a ceasefire in the west. It was now 2000hrs and events took another turn. Kluge received a message from Keitel stating that Hitler was alive and he changed his mind again. With Hitler alive the coup could not succeed, Kluge argued, and he wanted nothing more to do with it. When Stülpnagel and Hofacker arrived he reiterated his stance, which put Stülpnagel in a difficult position because he was well aware of the actions he had set in motion in Paris. Stülpnagel's only hope was that the success of his plan might change Kluge's mind. It did not. When he heard about events in Paris Kluge was furious. He relieved Stülpnagel of his command and ordered Blumentritt to cancel the order, but it was too late.

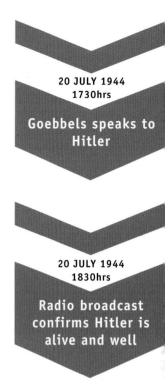

20 JULY 1944
1730hrs

Goebbels speaks to Hitler

20 JULY 1944
1830hrs

Radio broadcast confirms Hitler is alive and well

GENERALFELDMARSCHALL ERWIN ROMMEL

Rommel, commander-in-chief of Army Group B, was aware of plans to overthrow Hitler, but believed the timing of any coup was critical and that it should not be conducted before the Allied invasion. His logic was sound. In the spring of 1944 German troops in the west were convinced they could repel an Allied landing. If the Western Allies were defeated, Churchill and Roosevelt might have foregone their insistence upon an unconditional German surrender. To kill Hitler at such a time might have precipitated civil war, allowing the Soviets to capture most, if not all, of continental Europe.

Once the invasion had taken place and the Allies had secured a foothold, Rommel's thinking changed. It was clear they would soon break out of the bridgehead and that there was little or nothing to stop them reaching Germany. This being the case, he was happy to support an attempt on Hitler's life. He was set on this course when, on 17 July 1944, he was seriously injured in an air attack and was hospitalized.

When Rommel recovered he learned of the failed plot and the fallout. He was critical of Stauffenberg,

arguing that '... he had bungled it ... a front line soldier would have finished Hitler off' (quoted in Liddell Hart 1953: 486). This was a harsh appraisal and born out of the cruel treatment meted out to the conspirators by Hitler's henchmen. Rommel himself was not to escape.

After Rommel had been injured, Hitler wrote to him: 'Accept, Herr Field Marshal, my best wishes for your continued speedy recovery. Yours Adolf Hitler' (quoted in Liddell Hart 1953: 493). But his view of Rommel changed. In the purge that followed the 20 July Plot, Rommel was implicated. Hitler could not risk putting him in front of the People's Court, however, because the appearance of such a well-known and highly respected military leader might give succour to others who had reservations about the regime. Rommel would be offered a choice: suicide, followed by a full state funeral and the assurance that his name and his family would be protected; or, alternatively, he would be tried by the People's Court, which would result in his death, disgrace and penury for his family. He chose the former and on 14 October 1944 he committed suicide near his home in Ulm.

Boineburg-Lengsfeld had issued the order and, unlike in Berlin, it had been quickly and efficiently carried out. The barracks of the SS were surrounded and the occupants arrested and marched off to the Wehrmacht prison. Details of the night's events were secretly passed to SS-Oberführer Kurt Meyer, commander of 12. SS-Panzer-Division 'Hitlerjugend' and to SS-Obergruppenführer Sepp Dietrich, commander of I. SS-Panzerkorps, but they were too entangled in engagements with the Western Allies to help and could only pass on the information.

While the SS in Normandy was impotent. However, Kriegsmarine and Luftwaffe units in Paris were not, and when they heard of the coup attempt, their commanders threatened to liberate the SS men. This proved unnecessary though, as it was now clear the coup had failed and, in the early hours of 21 July, the order was given to release the prisoners. Some of the men who had been incarcerated thought their release was a trick and refused to leave, but it was genuine and, in an attempt to present a unified front, the army and the SS commanders agreed a set of words to explain the night's events. Kluge congratulated Hitler, and the army and SS men celebrated.

Berlin – the epicentre of the coup

Although support in the wider Reich was important, the key to the coup leaders' success lay in controlling the capital, Berlin. The conspirators needed to seize key points in the city and this was to be done by mobilizing units controlled by Generalleutnant Paul von Hase, the Berlin City Commandant, and those of Wehrkreis III, which covered Berlin and its environs. This would be difficult because, in order to reduce the chances of compromising the operation, the details of the coup were not known by all those involved; instead, it was believed that officers would follow orders. To complicate things further still, those units stationed in and around Berlin were often transferred to the front at very short notice, as were the officers in charge, so it was unclear from one month to the next what troops would be available and who would be in command.[10]

Wehrkreis III was commanded by General der Infanterie Joachim von Kortzfleisch, a Hitler loyalist and therefore unlikely to be supportive of the *Putsch*. Kortzfleisch was therefore in a pivotal position, and so the conspirators agreed that to leave him in post on the day of the coup was too much of a risk; it was decided that once Hitler had been assassinated Kortzfleisch would be invited to the Bendlerblock, arrested and replaced by an officer sympathetic to the coup.

On 20 July Kortzfleisch was sent for and arrived some time after 1700hrs. He expected to meet Fromm, but of course this was impossible and instead he was met by Beck, Hoepner and Olbricht. They explained what had happened but, as suspected, this staunch Nazi was not persuaded by the arguments presented by these luminaries. He refused to believe that Hitler was dead and indeed thought that this might be a coup. Unsurprisingly,

10 Troops based in Poland were also made ready to fly into Berlin, but they were not called for and returned to the front.

he refused to follow the *Valkyrie* orders and deploy his troops. He made to leave but realized this was impossible and so ran for the exit. After a chase, he was captured and incarcerated and was replaced by Generalleutnant Karl Freiherr von Thüngen.

Back in Wehrkreis III headquarters on the Hohenzollerndamm, it fell to Generalmajor Otto Herfurth, the chief of staff, to action the *Valkyrie* orders delivered by Major Hans Ulrich von Oertzen. Herfurth was relatively new in post and was not aware of the plan, unlike his predecessor Generalmajor Hans-Günther von Rost, who had been posted in March 1944, and who was part of the conspiracy. The responsibility for carrying out the orders, even with the help of Oertzen, did not sit easily with Herfurth and he called a council of war with his junior officers. Eventually Herfurth conceded that the orders were genuine and mobilized his units, comforted by the fact that it would take some time for them to reach their destination, by which stage things might be clearer. Some time after 1900hrs Thüngen arrived to take command, but as might be expected of someone who was previously the Inspekteur des Wehresatzwesens (Inspector of Recruiting) in Berlin, he was not proactive and did little to expedite the mobilization of the troops under his command.

The initial plan was to use two packs of explosives. However, Stauffenberg did not have time to prime both packs. As the plotters exited the Wolfsschanze, the spare explosive was discarded. It was later discovered by investigators. (NARA)

The units of Wehrkreis III were to seize a number of key buildings in the capital, including party offices, ministries (notably Propaganda and Interior), Gau Berlin headquarters and those of the Hitler-Jugend (Hitler Youth) and the Deutsche Arbeitsfront (DAF – German Labour Front). Importantly, they were also to secure the offices of the SS. However, as Herfurth had noted, it would take time for these units to reach the centre of Berlin; as if to highlight this fact, SS-Oberführer Humbert Achamer-Pifrader arrived at the Bendlerblock from Gestapo headquarters to arrest Stauffenberg and take him to see SS-Gruppenführer Heinrich Müller, head of the Gestapo, but Achamer-Pifrader was himself arrested by men loyal to Stauffenberg.

The two principal units of Wehrkreis III were Ersatz-Brigade 'Grossdeutschland' at Cottbus, some 80km south-east of Berlin, and the Infanterieschule (infantry school) at Döberitz, some 25km west of the city. Ersatz-Brigade 'Grossdeutschland' received news that the *Valkyrie* order had been enacted at about 1600hrs. Written confirmation arrived soon thereafter and Oberstleutnant Hans-Werner Stirius, in temporary command because Oberst Hermann Schulte-Heuthaus was on exercise, ordered that his men

Demolished concrete uprights from the main entrance to Gestapo headquarters, which were left after the clearing of the site (1957–63) still with remnants of the metal fittings. All the prisoners sent to the Gestapo headquarters passed through this gate. The remains now form part of the Topography of Terror Museum on Wilhelmstrasse. (Author)

move to the prearranged forming-up point just south of Berlin. When they arrived, one company was ordered to secure the Herzberg radio station (Deutschlandsender III), which it did by 1815hrs; another group was to seize the radio stations at Königswusterhausen (Deutschlandsender I) and Zeesen (Deutschlandsender II), which it did by 2000hrs, relieving troops from Panzertruppenschule II (Armour School II).

Generalleutnant Otto Hitzfeld, the commander of the infantry school, was also absent (on compassionate grounds) and the *Valkyrie* order was received by Oberst Albert Ringler. By 1800hrs advance reconnaissance parties were ready to move and Major Jakob, an infantry tactics officer, was ordered to occupy the Haus des Rundfunks (broadcasting house) in the Masurenallee. On arrival he deployed his troops to protect the facility and ordered that all broadcasts be stopped. He was assured that everything had been turned off, but not being an expert and having no signal officers to support him he could not confirm that this was the case. In fact, the studios and switch room had been moved to a bunker nearby and remained on air throughout.

Unaware of this, Jakob attempted to contact the Bendlerblock as ordered, to confirm that he had secured the broadcasting house, but the number he rang was not answered and therefore the plotters were never aware that he had been successful. Of more immediate concern for Major Jakob, however, was a unit of SS soldiers that had arrived on the scene. At first he attempted to place them under his command but they refused to comply and since the SS troops had also been deployed to guard the building, Jakob compromised and both units protected it, as this did not undermine his order. This uneasy alliance remained in place until late on 20 July, when Jakob was informed of what had happened; the following day he withdrew his troops.

Troops from the infantry school were also dispatched to the radio transmitter at Tegel and the overseas transmitter at Nauen. Both stations had been secured by 2100hrs, but again, with no signal experts to support the battle group, the officers in charge were never sure that transmissions had been stopped. Nor had word of their success filtered back to Döberitz. Oberst Müller of the OKH, who was based at the infantry school, attempted to energize the officers there; as far as he was aware the transmitters had not been secured and nothing had been done to seize the Oranienburg concentration camp as ordered. It had ben targeted by the plotters because it was an SS facility close to Berlin, and as such would have been a potential focal point for resistance to the coup.

The officers at the school had received conflicting messages concerning the day's events and the current situation, and were inclined not to execute the outstanding orders until they had written confirmation. Ringler eventually managed to contact Hitzfeld, who confirmed that the orders were legitimate, and at 2100hrs the troops moved out. At the same time Müller went to the Bendlerblock to seek permission from Olbricht to take command of the unit. He also asked that the troops allotted to secure the concentration camp be redirected to the Bendlerblock. Mertz von Quirnheim drafted the order and it was signed by Olbricht. He now made haste back to the infantry school, arriving at 2300hrs. However, when he arrived the junior officers at the school refused to act; they were now aware of the coup and that forces loyal to Hitler had regained the upper hand. At midnight the troops of the infantry school were ordered back to their barracks.

The vital transmitters

It is worth pausing at this point to discuss the importance of the signals officers. A key part of the plan was the seizure of the broadcasting house and the various radio transmitters dotted around the capital. All of them were captured, although the plotters at the Bendlerblock were not aware of the fact. More significantly, experts were needed to ensure that these facilities

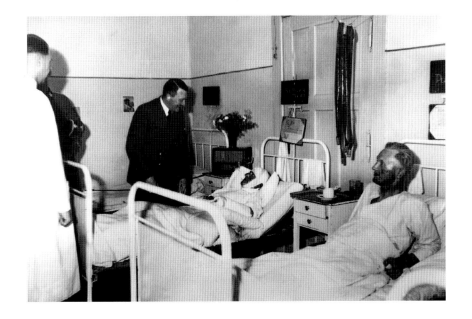

Hitler at the bedside of Kapitän zur See Heinz Assmann, who was injured in the blast of 20 July. In the next bed is Konteradmiral Karl-Jesko von Puttkamer, who was Hitler's naval liaison officer. He made a full recovery, and at the end of the war was sent to the Berghof to destroy Hitler's papers. (Topfoto)

were disabled. Initially it was planned that OKH would provide ten signals officers and OKW ten more. These were to be sent to the City Commandant's office where they would be directed to specific locations. However, Generalleutnant Thiele from OKW was aware that Hitler was alive and therefore would not supply the ten men he had promised. To make up the shortfall, Oberst Hassel (OKH) agreed to provide 20 signals officers. The signals officers were assembled but never ordered to any of the transmitters, radio stations or the broadcasting house, because they were not aware that these facilities had been captured. If they had been able to shut them down, the broadcasts detailing Hitler's survival might have been stopped, although there is no guarantee that this would have meant success for the coup.

The Berlin police

Another important force at the disposal of the conspirators was the Berlin Police Force. Early on 20 July, Major Egbert Hayessen of the General Army Office spoke to the Berlin Police President, Wolf Heinrich Graf von Helldorf. Hayessen was to act as liaison officer between the conspirators and the police to ensure they were ready to act when a state of emergency was declared. The police were intended to play a critical role in *Valkyrie*. They were to cooperate with the army and establish a series of raiding parties that would be led by police officers. These would each be allocated a Reich ministry with explicit direction to arrest ministers and other key figures. The police were also to support the army in closing roads and diverting traffic in the government quarter, and to set up roadblocks on the Berlin circular autobahn.

At about 1700hrs Helldorf arrived at the Bendlerblock and was briefed by Olbricht, who explained that the Wehrmacht had assumed power following the attempted assassination of the Führer. Before Helldorf left, Beck stressed that he might hear contradictory views from Nazis loyal to the old regime, which he was told to ignore. Helldorf returned to his headquarters on Alexanderstrasse and alerted the Security Police, but, as agreed with Olbricht, did not immediately mobilize his force. By 1900hrs Helldorf had still not received orders to move; he sent an aide to enquire what was happening, but by this time it was too late to do anything. A significant opportunity had been missed.

Initial success in Berlin

Within Berlin itself the mobilization was more successful, not least because many of the officers involved were aware of the plans and their troops had less distance to travel. Hase, the City Commandant of Berlin, was briefed by Major Egbert Hayessen on the morning of 20 July. It had originally been planned to brief him at least 24 hours ahead of the assassination attempt but this had not been possible because of the failed attempt on 15 July. In spite of the early notice, it was not until 1600hrs that Hase was telephoned with the second order detailing a state of emergency. Wach-Bataillon 'Grossdeutschland' was mobilized and ordered to move to Hase's headquarters on the Unter den Linden. The battalion's commanding officer, Major Otto Remer, and those of the other units under his command were also ordered to Hase's headquarters, where they would be given further orders. The first and most important briefing was to Remer, who was instructed, with his men, to secure the government quarter and arrest Goebbels. Wach-Bataillon 'Grossdeutschland' would later be reinforced by units from Armour School II and from other units in the Berlin garrison.

The conspirators recognized early on that armour would be critical to the success of the coup. Armour School II at Krampnitz possessed the most powerful and most mobile units; these were on a high alert to move, which meant that they were ideal for *Valkyrie*. However, the fact that they could be deployed at short notice also meant that it was impossible for the conspirators to plan with any certainty, because they could never be certain how many tanks and troops would be in Berlin when the blow was struck.

In spite of this uncertainty, Armour School II was given a key role in the coup, but for it to be decisive the tanks needed to roll as soon as news of Hitler's death reached Berlin. Yet it was not until 1600hrs that Oertzen contacted Oberst Wolfgang Gläsemer, Armour School II's commanding officer, informing him that a state of emergency existed and the army had taken control. Gläsemer was to direct the units under his command (including a battalion from the infantry cadets' training course and a battalion from the Unteroffiziersschule [NCO School] at Potsdam) to seize the radio transmitters at Königswusterhausen and Zeesen. They were also to reconnoitre the SS-Leibstandarte 'Adolf Hitler' barracks at Lichterfelde and deal with any resistance, but this proved unnecessary as the area was quiet. The rest of Gläsemer's units were to be concentrated at the Siegessäule (Victory Column) in the centre of Berlin. From here two battalions of troops were ordered to help secure the government quarter, while others protected the Bendlerblock. The rest of the units were to be held as a mobile reserve to deal with any other trouble, principally from the SS garrison commander's headquarters in Berlin. Once this was done, Gläsemer was ordered to report to the Bendlerblock, where he would receive further orders.

Martin Bormann, Hitler's personal secretary, and Göring, head of the Luftwaffe, discuss the damage to the conference room in the immediate aftermath of the explosion. They are accompanied by General der Flieger Bruno Loerzer of the Luftwaffe. To the right is the heavy map table that absorbed much of the blast. (Topfoto)

Although Gläsemer had enacted the first phase of the *Valkyrie* order, he was not comfortable with what was happening. The orders had been received by telephone and not in writing. Later John von Freyend, Keitel's aide, telephoned Gläsemer and stressed that orders from the Bendlerblock were not to be followed. This added to the sense of unease at Krampnitz and confirmation was sought from Generaloberst Heinz Guderian, Inspector General of Armoured Forces. However, he was unavailable and instead the call was taken by Oberst Ernst Bolbrinker. He in turn spoke to Olbricht, who confirmed the orders were correct, and this message was passed back to Gläsemer. Still not reassured, Gläsemer set off for the Bendlerblock; en route he was given news that an attempt had been made on Hitler's life, but he had survived and was well.

On arrival at the Bendlerblock, Gläsemer spoke to Olbricht in order to understand exactly what was going on. Olbricht confirmed that Hitler was dead and that Gläsemer was to follow the orders that Mertz von Quirnheim would issue to him. Gläsemer was not persuaded and refused to cooperate any further, stating that this was another stab in the back similar to that of 1918. He was immediately placed under house arrest.

The plan unravels

The units from Armour School II, now leaderless, pressed on towards their objectives and assembled at the Victory Column in the Tiergarten. However, by 2130hrs Guderian was aware of what was happening and Bolbrinker ordered the troops to move to the Fehrbelliner Platz, where he was based at the Inspectorate HQ, and not to follow any further orders from the Bendlerblock. By this time Wach-Bataillon 'Grossdeutschland' was similarly no longer following orders from the Bendlerblock, and Leutnant Hans Hagen, the unit *National Sozialistischer Führungs Offizier* (NSFO – National Socialist Leadership Officer), tried to bring the Armour School II units under his control, but he was told that they were only accepting orders from Guderian. Hagen reported this to Major Remer. Still unclear as to which side Guderian was on, Remer called Ersatz-Brigade 'Grossdeutschland' at Cottbus and asked for tanks and heavy weapons to be made available should they be needed to counter Guderian's force. This proved unnecessary; one of Remer's staff made contact with officers of Armour School II at the Fehrbelliner Platz, who confirmed Guderian's loyalty to the Führer.

Some time after 1600hrs Oberst Helmuth Schwierz, the commander of the Heeresfeuerwerkerschule (army pyrotechnical school), was informed that the *Valkyrie* order had been issued and that he was required to report to Hase's office. He was briefed on events and returned to Lichterfelde, where ten squads of 30 men

Entrance to the Propaganda Ministry on Mauerstrasse. This looks much as it did in July 1944. The front facade on Wilhelmstrasse was lost during redevelopment after the war. The building is now home to the Ministry of Labour and Social Affairs. (Author)

had been readied for deployment. The rest of the school's complement was ordered to remain at the Lichterfelde barracks under Schwierz's command to protect it against possible attack from the nearby SS garrison. The 300 troops who had been readied for action were placed under the command of Major Martin Korff and Hauptmann Alexander Maitre, and were ordered to move to the City Commandant's headquarters. There the two officers in charge received their orders. They were to secure the Propaganda Ministry and arrest Goebbels.[11] On arrival at the ministry, Maitre found it was already surrounded by troops of Remer's Wach-Bataillon 'Grossdeutschland'. Maitre made his way through the cordon and was informed that there had been an attempted coup and that Remer, under direct orders from the Führer, was in charge of the defence of Berlin. Maitre immediately placed his troops under Remer's command. When Korff was briefed on events he, too, supported a relieved Remer.

The mobilization of Heereswaffenmeisterschule I (Army Ordnance School I) was almost comical. Its commander, Generalmajor Walter Bruns, a supporter of the coup, received the *Valkyrie* order like the other commanders just after 1600hrs. His troops were readied to deploy into the city from Treptow, but the transport did not arrive and so they were obliged to move by foot or public tram. This they did, with Nr. 2 and Nr. 3 Kompanien occupying the Berliner Stadtschloss (Berlin City Castle). However, when they eventually arrived at about midnight, they encountered elements of Remer's battalion, which was no longer following the *Valkyrie* order. There was a slight contretemps, but unaware of developments the troops of army ordnance school I occupied the castle as ordered. Nr. 1 Kompanie, which had set off earlier than the other companies, had been redirected to the Bendlerblock and arrived there at 2145hrs. At about the same time, troops of Remer's battalion arrived. Both units had their orders, which were diametrically opposed, and a potentially explosive situation was only diffused when Nr. 1 Kompanie was persuaded to return to barracks.

Major Otto Remer

Wach-Bataillon 'Grossdeutschland' was commanded by Major Otto Remer, a former Hitler Youth leader and a Knight's Cross recipient. As Remer was known to be a staunch Nazi, it was suggested by the plotters that he be sent away on duty on the day of the coup, but Hase insisted that Remer would follow orders. On 20 July Remer attended the City Commandant's office on the Unter den Linden as directed and Hase showed him the area he was to secure. Remer understood and took leave to deploy his troops, who were in place by 1830hrs. However, Remer and his junior officers were already uneasy at what they had been asked to do, sensing that they were being used as part of a *Putsch*. Leutnant Hagen was particularly suspicious, because he believed he had seen Generalfeldmarschall von Brauchitsch earlier in the day in full uniform (Brauchitsch was a former army commander-in-chief) and

20 JULY 1944
1900hrs

Remer visits Goebbels and speaks to Hitler

20 JULY 1944
2000hrs

Witzleben visits Bendlerblock and speaks to Beck

11 The original thinking had been that Remer's men would arrest Goebbels, but this was thought too dangerous because the propaganda minister was also the honorary colonel of the unit.

asked Remer at around 1700hrs if he might speak to Goebbels to gain clarification of the situation. Remer agreed; he had, after all, complied with his orders, and Goebbels was honorary colonel of Remer's unit.

Hagen was duly seen by the propaganda minister and was persuaded of the gravity of the situation – troops were visible on the streets. Goebbels asked Hagen to invite Remer to see him to discuss the matter. Initially Hagen could not find Remer, but eventually he got word to him of the invitation. Unsure of who held legitimate power, Remer spoke to Hase, who insisted he was acting for the legal regime and that it was unclear where Goebbels stood. Remer was ordered to stay put. He was now torn between orders and a summons from the propaganda minister, and decided to speak to Goebbels, arriving at his office at around 1900hrs. Both parties explained what they knew and swore allegiance to the Führer. Now Goebbels played his trump card and put a call through to the Führer. Remer was given the receiver and asked if he recognized Hitler's voice. He did. Hitler now instructed him to deal with the insurrection until Himmler, as the new commander-in-chief of the Replacement Army, arrived.

Remer now ordered the troops who were guarding the government quarter to gather in the garden of Goebbels' residence, where the propaganda minister addressed them. He explained what had happened and Remer confirmed that he had personally been directed to crush the coup. Men of Wach-Bataillon 'Grossdeutschland' were redeployed to protect the area around the Propaganda Ministry, while others were positioned on key routes into the city to intercept units heading into the capital.

Oberleutnant Rudolf Schlee, commanding the troops protecting the Bendlerblock, was briefed on developments and it was made clear to him that only orders from Major Remer were to be obeyed. This direction

The Propaganda Ministry as it looks today. On 20 July 1944 Goebbels was in residence and in the evening it was surrounded by Major Remer's troops as part of Operation *Valkyrie*. In this building Remer took a call from Hitler and afterwards marched on the Bendlerblock to arrest the conspirators. (Amy Short)

ran counter to orders emanating from the building behind, and Schlee asked to speak to Olbricht. Olbricht was not available so he spoke instead to Mertz von Quirnheim, who insisted he was not to follow Remer's orders. Mertz von Quirnheim now retired to brief Olbricht on this serious development, and Schlee took the opportunity to slip out of the building. It was clear something was amiss and his suspicions were confirmed by another officer inside the building; the leaders of the coup were in the Bendlerblock. Schlee passed this news to Remer who was with Goebbels. The propaganda minister immediately phoned Hitler who directed that Remer's unit round up the conspirators. On returning to the Bendlerblock, Schlee secured all the entrances and prepared to enter the building. However, within the building 'loyal' German officers had now begun to take matters into their own hands.

The coup fails

At 1242hrs on 20 July an explosion had ripped through the briefing room at the Wolfsschanze where Hitler was being informed about developments on the Eastern Front. The reverberations of the bomb blast spread from the forests of East Prussia to all parts of the Reich, but now, as night came on, the coup everywhere began to implode.

Generalfeldmarschall von Witzleben had established himself at Zossen ready to take up his new role as Supreme Commander of the Armed Forces. However, it soon became clear that all was not going well in the attempt to wrest power from the Nazis. Wagner was now aware that Hitler was still alive and briefed Witzleben accordingly. Dismayed, Witzleben now travelled back to the Bendlerblock, arriving at about 2000hrs. He discussed the unfolding events with Beck and then Stauffenberg was called in to confirm Hitler's death, which he did. Witzleben was unconvinced, but he was sure

Steps leading down to the courtyard in the Bendlerblock. Today they take visitors to the German Resistance Memorial Centre where they can view all the facets of the resistance to Hitler, including the 20 July Plot. On the night of 20/21 July the conspirators were taken down these stairs to the courtyard to be shot. (Author)

The courtyard of the Bendlerblock as it is today. On the left is the entrance to the courtyard from Stauffenbergstrasse and on the right is the entrance to German Resistance Memorial Centre. In the foreground is part of the memorial to those killed there on 21 July 1944. (Author)

20 JULY 1944
2250hrs

Conspirators and Hitler loyalists exchange fire in the Bendlerblock

20 JULY 1944
2330Hrs

Beck commits suicide

about two things: firstly the inability of the conspirators to secure the government quarter and incarcerate the leading Nazis was a major failing. More significant, however, was the plotters' seeming inability to capture the broadcasting house and the various radio transmitters around the capital. Irrespective of whether the Führer was alive or dead, Witzleben explained, it was critical for the conspirators to keep the Nazis off the air and at the same time broadcast their message to the masses. Having vigorously made his point, and realizing all was lost, he returned to Zossen to await his fate.

As if to emphasise the point, at about 1700hrs the Nazis had made a radio broadcast announcing that an unsuccessful attempt had been made on Hitler's life. This was not widely received and it was not until 1830hrs that the first announcement was made on the German home service radio. Thereafter it was repeated on a number of occasions, ensuring that as wide an audience as possible was aware that Hitler was alive and well. At 2200hrs the Nazis issued a further radio message: 'For the second time in this war started by Jewry, a foul and murderous attempt has been made on our Führer's life … Providence protected the man who holds in his hands the destiny of the German people. The Führer remained unhurt…'. The message

rambled on before concluding, '"With the Führer – to victory." That is the slogan of the German people …' (quoted in Noakes 2010: 624).

At Wehrkreis III headquarters on the Hohenzollerndamm, Thüngen and Herfurth considered what to do next. At about 2000hrs Hase also arrived. He phoned Olbricht, who insisted that Thüngen act, but he was reluctant to and, after speaking to Generalleutnant Burgdorf, Thüngen addressed his staff and directed that orders from the Bendlerblock were to be ignored. Soon after he started to cancel the orders he had issued earlier and at 2230hrs Thüngen left the headquarters and did not return.

Hase returned to his office on the Unter den Linden just after 2100hrs and received a call from General der Infanterie Hermann Reinecke, whom Keitel had now put in charge of troops in Berlin. Reinecke ordered Hase to make arrangements for all of the troops in the capital to be placed under his command so that they could be deployed against hostile forces in the Bendlerblock.

Hase in turn contacted Remer and ordered him to return to the City Commandant's headquarters, but Remer refused, insisting that he was now only following orders from the Führer. Indeed, Remer insisted that Hase come to Goebbels' house, which he did. Hase explained he had been relieved of his command and that Remer's troops should now report to Reinecke. Goebbels in turn explained that Remer was personally responsible to the Führer for restoring order in the capital and as such would not submit himself to Reinecke. The meeting concluded and, having discharged his orders, Hase asked if he might have something to eat. He stayed for dinner before later being arrested.

Back in the Bendlerblock, forces loyal to Hitler were gradually tightening the noose on the conspirators. Although incarcerated, Generaloberst Fromm had managed to make contact with the outside world via an infrequently used door in his improvised prison cell that – amazingly – was not guarded. Using this exit his aide, Rittmeister Heinz-Ludwig Bartram, contacted forces loyal to Hitler and ordered that they take steps to arrest the conspirators and free Fromm. At the same time, Fromm considered the possibility of escaping using this route, but he saw little benefit in this. It would be difficult

Headstone in the Alter Sankt Matthäus Kirchhof. This cemetery, a short distance from the Bendlerblock, is where Beck, Olbricht, Stauffenberg, Mertz von Quirnheim and Haeften were originally buried. Their bodies were later exhumed and cremated. (Author)

After the unsuccessful assassination attempt on 20 July 1944, Hitler made a radio broadcast to the nation to reassure the people that he was fit and well. His audience at the Wolfsschanze consisted of his closest advisors, including Hitler's personal adjutant, SS-Grüppenführer Julius Schaub, in front of the curtains. (Topfoto)

for a Generaloberst to get out of the building unnoticed, and it would be dangerous. In any case, Fromm believed he would soon be released.

Completely separately, and unknown to Fromm, a number of officers in the building were becoming increasingly concerned by the conflict between messages they were receiving from the radio and those coming out of Olbricht's office. The senior officer in this group, Oberstleutnant Franz Herber, arranged a meeting with Olbricht to establish the truth. At 2100hrs the officers met Olbricht but he was not able to persuade them with his answers. Unconvinced, they ignored his order to help guard the building and instead they went to Oberstleutnant Bolko von der Heyde's office to discuss their next move. Though armed with weapons from the magazine, they decided against direct action but instead would press Olbricht for straight answers. Olbricht was once again evasive, explaining that he had received word that Hitler was dead but was equally aware of the broadcasts that stated the Führer was alive.

The conversation was interrupted by a shot outside, which led to a more general melee. As Herber came out of Olbricht's office he was shot at by Hauptmann Friedrich Klausing (who had been Stauffenberg's adjutant in Haeften's absence during the latter's leave), and Herber in turn returned fire. Stauffenberg, though clearly handicapped, pressed a pistol to his side and fired at Oberstleutnant Karl Pridun. Further shots were exchanged and Stauffenberg was hit in the left shoulder. Losing blood, he made his way to Fromm's office. Here he met up with the prime movers of the coup, Olbricht, Hoepner, Beck, Mertz von Quirnheim and Haeften – who was busy burning incriminating evidence. It was plain that the game was up, and they submitted to Herber and his men.

Meanwhile, Fromm, who had sought and been granted permission to move to his apartment, was briefed on events and made his way to his office. When he arrived the conspirators were being held at gunpoint. He ordered that they be disarmed and declared that they would be tried by court martial. Beck asked that he might keep his pistol so that he could commit suicide; Fromm acceded and Beck placed the weapon to his forehead and pulled the trigger. The bullet only grazed him and he fired again. Badly injured, he fell to the floor but he was still alive and a soldier from Wach-Bataillon 'Grossdeutschland' was ordered to deliver the *coup de grâce*. While this was going on Hoepner and Olbricht asked for the opportunity to write their final testament, a request to which Fromm agreed, but when after 30 minutes they still had not finished he lost patience and called the 'court' to order; the conspirators were all to be executed.

Stauffenberg maintained that he was the ringleader and that the others had only followed orders; Fromm was silent and motioned that they should be taken away. Hoepner stepped forward and asked to speak to Fromm in private. When they returned Fromm directed that Hoepner be spared and instead be taken to prison.

Bartram arranged a firing squad in the courtyard of the Bendlerblock. Ten men were identified and assembled in front of a number of lorries whose lights were used to illuminate the pile of sand, in front of which the condemned men were to be killed. Olbricht was shot first and then it was to be Stauffenberg, but as the second volley was fired Haeften threw himself in the way. At the same time Stauffenberg, in one last show of defiance, called out 'Long Live Holy Germany,' before he too was gunned down. Last in line was Mertz von Quirnheim, the unassuming Oberst who had done so much to galvanize the coup.

Fromm now addressed the troops and closed with three rousing 'Sieg Heils' before heading off to see Goebbels. The lifeless bodies were loaded onto a lorry and taken to the nearby Alter Sankt Matthäus Kirchhof Cemetery in Schöneberg, where they were buried. When Hitler found out that the conspirators had been executed and buried he was furious and ordered that they be disinterred. Their bodies were burnt and the ashes scattered to the four winds.

At about the same time at the Wolfsschanze, Hitler's personal staff were gathered together along with the walking wounded to watch their leader deliver a broadcast to the nation using equipment hastily sourced from Königsberg. In his opening remarks he confirmed that there had been an attempt on his life by Oberst Graf von Stauffenberg and that a number of people had been killed or injured by the blast but that he was well. He went on: 'At a time when the German armies are engaged in a very tough struggle, a very small group ... thought they could stab us in the back just like in November 1918. But this time they have made a very big mistake ...'. He stressed that the group was not representative of the Wehrmacht and that this 'small criminal clique will now be mercilessly exterminated'. He concluded that 'the finger of fate [is] pointing me towards the continuation of my work and so I shall carry on with it' (quoted in Noakes 2010: 624–26).

Overleaf:
As the shadows lengthened on 20 July, the conspirators found themselves in an increasingly desperate situation. All across the Reich and in Berlin the Nazis were re-establishing their authority. In the Bendlerblock itself a number of officers, led by Oberstleutnant Franz Herber, confronted General Olbricht to understand what was happening. Unconvinced by the response they decided to act. This culminated in an exchange of fire between officers loyal to the conspirators and those loyal to the regime. Stauffenberg himself became involved and though he only had one hand he was able to return fire before he was hit in the left shoulder. Losing blood he retired to Fromm's office where he joined the rest of the conspirators. They were disarmed and Fromm ordered a summary court martial in his office. The ringleaders – Stauffenberg, Haeften, Mertz von Quirnheim, Olbricht and Beck – were sentenced to death. Beck was allowed to commit suicide; the others were taken out to the courtyard and were executed.

AFTERMATH

Hitler's vengeance

The shots that rang out in the courtyard of the Bendlerblock in the early hours of 21 July signalled not the end, but the beginning of the bloodletting. Investigations led by the RSHA uncovered more and more names associated with the conspiracy. Many of the officers identified were from the old ruling class and some in the Nazi Party saw this as an opportunity to eliminate the traditional elites. Robert Ley, the leader of the DAF, spoke of 'blue-blooded swine whose entire families must be wiped out' (quoted in Grunberger 1974: 189), while Goebbels, who was unusually restrained, simply issued directives for the post-war liquidation of the aristocracy. Hitler was similarly outraged

Entrance to the Alter Sankt Matthäus Kirchhof. On the night of 20/21 July, Fromm ordered the bodies of Beck, Olbricht, Stauffenberg, Mertz von Quirnheim and Haeften be taken here and buried with full military honours. The cemetery is the resting place of the Brothers Grimm and other notable Germans, though the conspirators were not to rest in peace there for long. (Author)

and wanted revenge, but ordered them to desist with such rhetoric; he insisted on a more measured approach. The conspirators would be tracked down by SS-Obergruppenführer Kaltenbrunner, the RSHA chief, and SS-Gruppenführer Müller, the head of the Gestapo.

Yet although Himmler and Kaltenbrunner were sent to Berlin immediately after the bombing to start their investigation, some of the conspirators had already escaped the net. Stauffenberg, Olbricht, Haeften and Mertz von Quirnheim had been summarily shot and Beck had taken his own life. General der Artillerie Wagner also committed suicide, as did Major von Oertzen, who had transmitted the *Valkyrie* order. He had been detained soon after the plot, but had been released and went home, where he killed himself just as the Gestapo arrived to re-arrest him.

On the Eastern Front, Tresckow heard the news of the coup's failure from his aide Schlabrendorff. Convinced that he would be identified as one of the conspirators, he explained that he would take his own life in order not to incriminate anyone else under torture. Schlabrendorff tried to dissuade him but Tresckow was not for turning. He made his way to the front and committed suicide. When his body was recovered it was assumed he had been killed by the enemy and his body was taken back to Germany to be buried. Later his role in the plot was uncovered and his body was exhumed and taken to the crematorium of Sachsenhausen concentration camp.

In France, Stülpnagel, whose role in the plot had been exposed to those in the Wolfsschanze by Kluge, was recalled to Germany. Understanding the meaning of this order he set off, but stopped en route near Verdun where he had served in World War I. He slipped away from his staff with his pistol with the intention of killing himself, but the head shot was not fatal and only served to blind him. He was rescued by his aides and treated in hospital. Meantime, Kluge's treachery meant he initially escaped suspicion, but on

Those involved in the trial of the 20 July plotters give the Nazi salute. Nearest the camera is *Volksgerichtsrat* Paul Lämmle. In the centre is the president, Roland Freisler, and to his right is General der Infanterie Hermann Reinecke, head of the *Allgemeines Wehrmachtsamt*. (Topfoto)

**21 JULY 1944
0030hrs**

**Olbricht,
Stauffenberg,
Mertz von
Quirnheim and
Haeften executed**

**21 JULY
1944**

**Tresckow commits
suicide**

17 August he was relieved of his command after apparently trying to contact the Allied High Command. On his way back to Germany he followed much the same route as Stülpnagel, the man he had betrayed. He too took a break on the journey near Verdun and swallowed a poison capsule, which proved more effective than had Stülpnagel's pistol.

Those officers who decided not to take their own lives presumably believed that if they were arrested they would come before a military court. But Hitler was determined that they would not be tried by their own kind and instead would appear in the *Volksgericht* or People's Court. Thus officers suspected of disloyalty were hunted down and arraigned before a military tribunal. These were headed by officers chosen by Hitler and included Generalfeldmarschall Gerd von Rundstedt, Keitel and Guderian. In the first hearing 22 senior officers were discharged from the army, including Witzleben, Hoepner, Hase and Stieff. Stripped of rank they were tried on 7 August in the People's Court by Judge-President Roland Freisler, who sought to demean them at every turn. Witzleben was particularly harshly treated; his false teeth were removed and his belt and braces were confiscated so that he had to hold his trousers up with his hands. The proceedings were filmed and shown to public audiences in an effort to ensure similar treasonable acts were not repeated. The four were sentenced to death by hanging and sent to Plötzensee Prison, where the sentence was to be carried out. On 8 August these four and four others were strung up on meat hooks until they died. The whole episode was photographed for the Führer. Two days later, Fellgiebel and Stauffenberg's older brother Berthold was executed in the same way.

Schlabrendorff, who had tried to dissuade Tresckow from taking his own life, was arrested and sent to Gestapo headquarters in Berlin, where he was incarcerated with Admiral Wilhelm Canaris, former director of the Abwehr; Hans Oster, Canaris's chief of staff; Carl Friedrich Goerdeler, former mayor

Generalfeldmarschall Erwin von Witzleben, now stripped of his army uniform and rank, appears at the People's Court in August 1944. To further embarrass Witzleben, his belt and braces were removed so forcing him to hold his trousers up. He was found guilty and executed on 8 August 1944. (Topfoto)

of Leipzig; and the theologian Dietrich Bonhoeffer. Schlabrendorff suffered terrible torture but bravely resisted, implicating only Tresckow, who was now safe from the Gestapo. His resilience saved his life. Not until February 1945 did Schlabrendorff appear before the People's Court and, as luck would have it, his case was interrupted by an air raid. Everyone made their way to the shelters except for Freisler, who went back to get Schlabrendorff's file, which was still in the courtroom. At the same time the building was hit by a bomb and Freisler was killed – an example of divine intervention if ever there was one. The case was adjourned and when it was reconvened Schlabrendorff was acquitted. He was later re-arrested, but survived the war.

Canaris, Oster and Bonhoeffer were not so lucky. After months of torture they were killed in Flossenbürg concentration camp on 9 April as the SS guards, in one last orgy of violence, 'cleansed' the facility before US troops arrived. Goerdeler was hanged in February and was one of the many civilians to perish. A number of the so-called Kreisau Circle, who sympathized with the conspirators, were also executed, including the leader of the group Helmut von Moltke and the diplomat Adam von Trott zu Solz. Even those unassociated with the plot were not immune, such was the paranoia: 'During the wave of persecution that followed the Officers' Plot, an Evangelical deaconess was executed for describing Himmler, the newly appointed C-in-C of the reserve army [Replacement Army], as "a man of simple background not sprung from the soldierly estate"' (Grunberger 1974: 189).

But it was the officer class that suffered the greatest retribution. Having recovered sufficiently to face trial, Stülpnagel went before the People's Court on 30 August, along with other senior officers in France including Stauffenberg's cousin, Oberst Cäsar von Hofacker. All had resolutely defied their torturers and, indeed, Hofacker led a spirited defence in his trial, but this simply resulted in a further term in prison. During this time he revealed,

2 FEBRUARY
1945

Goerdeler executed

12 MARCH
1945

Fromm executed

A close-up of the special beam that was inserted in the execution room in Plötzensee Prison. The beam is fitted with a series of hooks and from these the condemned were hanged, including Generalfeldmarschall Erwin von Witzleben, Generaloberst Erich Hoepner, Generalleutnant Paul von Hase and Generalmajor Helmuth Stieff. (Author)

under duress, a conversation he had with Rommel about impressing on Hitler the need to end the war. This confession, together with other evidence, brought into question Rommel's loyalty. The days of the Desert Fox were now numbered; it was simply a question of whether he would be executed or would die by his own hand.

The decision of a number of the conspirators to commit suicide and the silence of others, in spite of lengthy and brutal torture, meant that a number of individuals escaped punishment. Generalleutnant Adolf Heusinger, who had been at the 20 July briefing, was arrested but not tortured and, with no concrete evidence of involvement in the plot, he was released. He survived the war and later became a senior figure in NATO. Generalmajor Hans Speidel, Rommel's chief of staff, was also arrested but with help from Guderian was released and, like Heusinger, became a top NATO commander after the war.

Changes in the Nazi hierarchy

Both Heusinger and Speidel were dismissed and these departures, along with the executions, left yawning gaps in the senior ranks of the army. Hitler acted quickly to fill these vacancies. Guderian retained the job of Inspector General of Armoured Forces but additionally became Chief of the Army General Staff, replacing Generaloberst Kurt Zeitzler, who had left the job in early July due to nervous exhaustion. His promotion, however, was due more to his loyalty to Hitler than his skill as a commander. Although he was a gifted tactician and had been instrumental in the development of *Blitzkrieg*, he was no strategist. As such he was little more than a figurehead; a mouthpiece for Hitler. In France, Generalfeldmarschall Walter Model replaced Kluge, but at the end of August Rundstedt returned to take command of Heeresgruppe D (Army Group D); Model retained command of Army Group B. Generalmajor Wilhelm Burgdorf was promoted Generalleutnant and made head of the Army Personnel Office following the death of Schmundt.

The memorial at Plötzensee Prison to those who died at the hands of the Nazis. Today Plötzensee is still a working prison but this part has been isolated and houses the memorial and a small exhibition. (Author)

Lackeys like Jodl and Keitel – whose nickname was Lakeitel[12] – retained their place in the inner circle. Indeed, such was their blind obedience to the cause that after the event Keitel was 'incapable of recognizing the conflict in which the conspirators of 20 July 1944 find themselves, and saw there nothing but injured pride, frustrated ambition and office-seeking! When Rundstedt was asked in Nuremberg whether he had never thought of getting rid of Hitler, he replied firmly and unhesitatingly that he was a soldier, not a traitor' (Fest 1979: 368). In spite of this unwavering loyalty, the conspiracy undoubtedly heightened Hitler's mistrust of the army and increasingly he surrounded himself with officers from the Kriegsmarine and the Luftwaffe, regardless of the fact that these arms of the Wehrmacht played little or no part in the fighting at the end of the war.

The power of the SS also grew. Himmler was appointed as commander of the Replacement Army superseding Fromm, who had been expelled from the army in September 1944 and who was executed in March 1945 for cowardice – no evidence was provided for his complicity in the plot. Himmler was now responsible for raising new formations, mostly *Volksgrenadier-Divisionen*. The prefix '*Volk*' was deliberate and was designed to differentiate the new units from established army units commanded by the old officer corps. These new divisions were administered by the SS and only officers approved by the SS could serve in these units. However, such were the shortages of suitable candidates that officers were removed from the army and posted to the SS, often against their will, in order to fill technical posts that no one in the SS had the skills to do.

However, although Himmler gained powers, paradoxically, he lost influence, because the new roles took him away from the Führer. In his absence questions were asked about Himmler's competence. He was after all the head of security, which had failed to uncover the 20 July Plot. The true winner in the power struggle that developed after the 20 July Plot was Martin Bormann. As Hitler's private secretary he was continually at the Führer's side. He controlled the party and access to Hitler. Goebbels still retained his position, and Bormann knew better than to argue with him, but Bormann had 'achieved an undisputed supremacy such as had never been previously known in the immediate entourage of his master' (Trevor-Roper 2002: 32).

In this power struggle Göring became an increasingly peripheral figure and, in an effort to curry favour, Keitel and he, as heads of their respective services, suggested that the military salute be replaced by the Nazi salute and a 'Heil Hitler!' The idea was presented as being 'the desire and the demand of all Services …'. Göring went on to suggest that it was an 'indication of unshakeable loyalty to the Führer and of the close bonds of comradeship between Wehrmacht and Party' (Warlimont n.d.: 442). The change was instituted on 23 July 1944 and woe betide anyone who failed to follow the new order. General der Panzertruppe Fridolin von Senger und Etterlin, the defender of Monte Cassino, was criticized for not making the 'German

12 From the German *Lakai* – lackey.

9 APRIL 1945

Canaris and Oster executed

Greeting'. This was symptomatic of a wider unease that permeated the army after 20 July. Officers suspected of disloyalty were condemned by political officers (NSFOs) in the Wehrmacht. Indeed, an anonymous complaint from someone with a grievance was often sufficient for an officer to be reduced to the ranks, or worse. This terror continued until the end of the war and, as such, the officer corps was decimated at a time when it needed to be maintained to cope with the military emergencies engulfing the Reich.

The attack on the army went further. On 24 July an order was issued that stipulated that, before an officer could be posted into a new job, he and his family should be vetted. A week later, on 1 August, the so-called *Sippenhaft* (literally, kin liability) was introduced. This meant that families of personnel in the armed forces were held personally responsible for their actions. If their menfolk did not do their duty then their relations could be imprisoned or executed. This would ensure that men at the front would obey orders, no matter how futile.

For Hitler, then, the conspiracy offered an opportunity to destroy his enemies and re-establish his authority over the army. At the same time, this treachery was used to explain military reverses that might otherwise have been blamed on Hitler. But while Hitler had taken the opportunity to turn this attack to his advantage, it came at a cost. The explosion on 20 July had killed stenographer Dr Heinz Berger and, on 22 July, General der Flieger (literally, General of the Flyers) Günther Korten and Oberst Heinz Brandt also died. Ironically, the latter was a resistance sympathizer. On 1 October Generalleutnant Schmundt died as a result of the injuries he received. Perversely, those injured in the blast were awarded a special wound badge with a 20 July 1944 inscription.

The headline in the *Völkischer Beobachter*, the official Nazi newspaper, on the day after the coup attempt. It reads 'Long Live the Führer – Unsuccessful assassination attempt on the Führer by hostiles'. (Author)

The consequences for Hitler

Hitler himself had escaped from the briefing largely unscathed. However, as time passed it was clear that the blast had taken its toll on the Führer's health. Both his eardrums had been perforated, which affected his hearing and his balance. The right ear continued to bleed and had to be cauterized. His right arm was still painful, made worse by Morell's treatment, which made shaking hands or even signing documents difficult. Headaches kept him awake at night and he was prescribed cocaine, which relieved many of his symptoms. However, somewhat unusually, the blast did seem to have cured Hitler's tremor, at least in the short term.

The bomb attack also heightened Hitler's paranoia, and precautions were taken to prevent a repeat. An investigation undertaken by the RSHA concluded that the previous security precautions could not prevent a general staff officer who had been invited to deliver a brief from an assassination attempt. After 20 July, officers were frisked and no weapons could be brought into briefings. Briefcases were checked, much to Warlimont's chagrin, and in the end he stopped bringing one. After being checked for bombs, the filter system in Hitler's bunker was overhauled along with the back-up oxygen system to ensure they were fit for purpose. Both were in need of improvement and more cylinders of oxygen were supplied to allow 30 days' use. To prevent poisoning, Hitler's food was now tasted.

Security was also tightened in the headquarters. Immediately after the blast FHQ Wolfsschanze was swamped with SS personnel. Elements of the SS-Leibstandarte 'Adolf Hitler' arrived on the night of 20/21 July and occupied key points. Their presence, however,

The cause of the blast was initially unclear. However, it soon became apparent that explosives had been used. The remains of Stauffenberg's briefcase were recovered from the shattered briefing room and pieced together. (NARA)

caused friction with the normal security personnel and eventually they were withdrawn. But it was clear that changes needed to be made and so more SS and RSD personnel were stationed in Sperrkreis I. Traudl Junge complained that 'There were barriers and new guard posts everywhere, mines, tangles of barbed wire, watchtowers. The paths along which I had walked my dog one day would suddenly be blocked the next with a guard wanting to see my pass' (Junge 2004: 146). There was also a shake-up in the command structure at FHQ Wolfsschanze. Major, now Oberst, Remer, who had shown his undivided loyalty to the Führer in Berlin on 20 July, was made responsible for security inside and outside the headquarters. Oberst Streve was effectively demoted and was now only camp commandant. All the headquarters troops he had commanded were transferred to Remer. Hitler opined, 'How thankful I am to Remer … a few more fine, clear-thinking officers like him and I wouldn't have to worry about the future' (quoted in Irving 2002: 712).

CONCLUSION

The 20 July Plot was the last genuine effort to assassinate Hitler. In the dying days of the war, Albert Speer, Minister of Armaments and War Production, considered gassing him in the Berlin bunker. Not without some difficulty he sourced the materials, but in the end he abandoned his plan. Hitler took his own life on 30 April and the war in Europe ended a week later. If Stauffenberg had been successful it is questionable if the war would have ended any sooner. Certainly Churchill was undecided. In the immediate aftermath he showed his disappointment at the failure of the plot when he commented, 'They missed the old bugger.' However, on reflection, he provided a more measured response, which he delivered to the House of Commons on 28 September 1944:

> When Herr Hitler escaped his bomb on July 20th he described his survival as providential; I think that from a purely military point of view we can all agree with him, for certainly it would be most unfortunate if the Allies were to be deprived, in the closing phases of the struggle, of that form of warlike genius by which Corporal Schicklgruber[13] has so notably contributed to our victory. (Hansard HC Deb, Vol. 403, c. 482)

Other commentators considered the very real possibility of a civil war in the aftermath of a successful attempt on Hitler's life and others questioned whether the plotters' plan to agree a separate peace with the Western Allies was feasible. In truth, it was very unlikely in light of the agreement made at Casablanca in 1943, in spite of the fact that Churchill was becoming increasingly concerned by the threat posed by Communism in a post-war Europe.

This is all conjecture, however. Stauffenberg detonated his bomb, but it failed to kill Hitler. The coup was crushed and the conspirators fully

---

13 Hitler's father, Alois, changed the family name from 'Schicklgruber' to 'Hitler' in 1876, 13 years before Adolf was born.

HIER STARBEN
FÜR
DEUTSCHLAND
AM 20. JULI 1944

GENERALOBERST LUDWIG BECK
GENERAL DER INFANTERIE FRIEDRICH OLBRICHT
OBERST CLAUS GRAF SCHENK VON STAUFFENBERG
OBERST ALBRECHT RITTER MERTZ VON QUIRNHEIM
OBERLEUTNANT WERNER VON HAEFTEN

In the courtyard of the Bendlerblock a plaque has been mounted, which reads 'Here died for Germany on 20 July 1944 – Beck, Olbricht, Stauffenberg, Mertz and Haeften'. On the anniversary of the coup a wreath is hung. (Author)

understood the consequences. In a note written shortly before 20 July, Stauffenberg noted that 'It is time for something to be done. Yet he who dares to do something must be aware that he is likely to go down in German history as a traitor. If he failed to do the deed, however, he would be a traitor to his own conscience'. In the immediate aftermath of the attack he was seen by many as a traitor, and even after the war Stauffenberg and the other conspirators were viewed as such. However, gradually public perceptions changed and, in 1953, a memorial was established in the Bendlerblock courtyard and a headstone was erected at the Alter Sankt Matthäus Kirchhof Cemetery. Perhaps most poignant, though, is the memorial service held each 20 July to recognize the sacrifice of these brave individuals.

BIBLIOGRAPHY

Baigent, M. & Leigh, R., *Secret Army: Stauffenberg and the Mystical Crusade Against Hitler*, Arrow Book, London (2006)

Baur, H., *Hitler At My Side*, Eichler Publishing Corporation, Houston, TX (1986)

Below, N. von, *At Hitler's Side: The Memoirs of Hitler's Luftwaffe Adjutant 1937–45*, Greenhill Books, London (2004)

Bracher, K. D., *The German Dictatorship*, Penguin Books, London (1988)

Bullock, A., *Hitler – A Study in Tyranny*, Pelican Books, London (1962)

Fest, J., *Hitler*, Weidenfeld & Nicolson, London (1974)

Fest, J., *Inside Hitler's Bunker – The Last Days of the Third Reich*, Pan Books, London (2005)

Fest, J., *The Face of the Third Reich*, Penguin Books, London (1979)

Focken, C., *FHQ Führerhauptquartiere – Wolfsschanze (Ostpreussen)*, Helios Verlag, Aachen (2008)

Gisevius, H. B., *Valkyrie: An Insider's Account of the Plot to Kill Hitler*, Da Capo Press, Cambridge, MA (2009)

Grunberger, R., *A Social History of the Third Reich*, Pelican Books, London (1974)

Hansard HC Deb, Vol. 403, c. 482

Hoffmann, P., *The History of German Resistance 1933–1945*, McGill-Queen's University Press, Montreal and Kingston (1996)

Hoffmann, P., *Hitler's Personal Security: Protecting the Führer, 1921–1945*, Da Capo Press, Cambridge, MA (2000)

Hoffmann, P., *Stauffenberg: A Family History, 1905–1944*, McGill-Queen's University Press, Montreal and Kingston (2008)

Irving, D., *Hitler's War and the War Path*, Focal Point Publications, London (2002)

Johnson, A. L., *Hitler's Military Headquarters – Organization, Structures, Security and Personnel*, R. James Bender Publishing, San Jose, CA (1999)

Jones, N., *Countdown to Valkyrie: The July Plot to Assassinate Hitler*,

Frontline Books, London (2008)

Junge, T., *Until the Final Hour: Hitler's Last Secretary*, Phoenix, London (2004)

Kershaw, I., *Luck of the Devil: The Story of Operation Valkyrie*, Penguin Books, London (2009)

Kershaw, I., *The End: Hitler's Germany 1944–45*, Allen Lane, London (2011)

Liddell Hart, B. H. (ed.), *The Rommel Papers*, Collins Press, London (1953)

Linge, H., *With Hitler to the End: The Memoirs of Adolf Hitler's Valet*, Frontline Books, London (2009)

McDonough, F., *Opposition and Resistance in Nazi Germany*, Cambridge University Press, Cambridge (2001)

Mommsen, H., *Germans Against Hitler: The Stauffenberg Plot and Resistance Under the Third Reich*, I. B. Tauris, London (2009)

Moorhouse, R., *Killing Hitler: The Third Reich and the Plots to Kill the Führer*, Vintage Books, London (2007)

Neumarker, U., Conrad, R. & Woywodt, C., *Wolfsschanze – Hitler's Machtzentrale im Zweiten Weltkrieg*, Ch Links Verlag, Berlin (2007)

Noakes, J. (ed.), *Nazism 1919–45 Vol. 4: The German Home Front in World War II*, University of Exeter Press, Exeter (2010)

Raiber, M. D., 'The Führerhauptquartiere', *After the Battle*, No. 19, 28–47 (1977)

Schrader, H., *Codename Valkyrie: General Friedrich Olbricht and the Plot Against Hitler*, Haynes Publishing, Sparkford (2009)

Schramm, W. R. von, *Conspiracy Among Generals*, George Allen & Unwin, London (n.d.)

Schroeder, C., *He Was My Chief: The Memoirs of Adolf Hitler's Secretary*, Frontline Books, London (2009)

Seaton, A., *The German Army 1933–1945*, St Martin's Press, New York, NY (1982)

Seidler, F. W. & Zeigert, D., *Hitler's Secret Headquarters*, Greenhill Books, London (2004)

Senger und Etterlin, General F. von, *Neither Fear Nor Hope*, Greenhill Books, London (1989)

Shirer, W. L., *The Rise and Fall of the Third Reich*, Secker & Warburg, London (1972)

Speer, A., *Inside the Third Reich*, Weidenfeld & Nicolson, London (1970)

Taylor, B., *Hitler's Headquarters: From Beer Hall to Bunker, 1920–1945*, Potomac Books, Washington, DC (2007)

Trevor-Roper, H. (ed.), *The Bormann Letters*, Weidenfeld & Nicolson, London (1954)

Trevor-Roper, H., *The Last Days of Hitler*, Pan Books, London (2002)

Warlimont, General der Artillerie W., *Inside Hitler's Headquarters 1939–45*, Presidio Press, Novato, CA (n.d.)

Zimmermann, E. & Jacobsen, H. A., *Germans Against Hitler July 20, 1944*, Berto-Verlag, Bonn (1960)

INDEX

References to illustrations are shown in **bold**.
Captions to plates are shown in (brackets).